HENRY COOPER

An Autobiography

Was ever a British boxer so loved by so many
millions as Henry Cooper? The boxing fans
adore him for the famous left hook called 'Enery's
'ammer', for putting Cassius Clay on the floor,
for never giving up, for being a British Heavyweight good enough to take on the world. But
Henry's fans include housewives who don't
know a jab from an uppercut, their husbands
and children, eminent statesmen, maiden ladies
who think boxing 'degrading', the entire
population of Eton College, the Arsenal Football
Club, the Royal Family—and all the rest of us.

Henry's warm-hearted, highly entertaining
autobiography will delight the millions who have
a firm place in their respect and affection for the
gentle giant whose humour, dignity, courage and
boxing skill brought honour to his sport and
pride to his countrymen. In a very special sense,
Henry Cooper was, is, and always will be *Our* Enery.

HENRY COOPER
AN AUTOBIOGRAPHY

CORONET BOOKS
Hodder Paperbacks Ltd., London

Printed and bound in Great Britain for
Coronet Books,
Hodder Paperbacks Ltd,
St. Paul's House, Warwick Lane,
London, EC4P 4AH
by Hazell Watson & Viney Ltd,
Aylesbury, Bucks

ISBN 0 340 17854 X

For
Jim Wicks

ACKNOWLEDGEMENTS

To Albina, Mum and Dad, my brother George, and my old trainer George Page my special gratitude. Also John Samuel, sports editor of *The Guardian*, for all his help and advice with the writing of this book. To all those others, named and unnamed in its pages, relatives, friends, and not least fans, my warmest thanks. Without them, each in different ways, I could not have achieved what I have.

H.C.

Wembley,
Middlesex
July 1972

ILLUSTRATIONS

between pages 96 and 97

CHAPTER ONE

We were born, George and me, on May 3, 1934, at the Lying-in Hospital, York Road, Westminster, the biggest surprise of my mother's life. She was going to call us Walter. But at the hospital they knew a bit more than they were ready to say. Mum was asked to go in six weeks before we were born, and one day the matron said : 'Would you like to see some X-rays of twins?'

My mother said she didn't mind and they showed her these films. It looked like a spine with eggs either side.

'Would you like twins?' the matron asked.

'Oh, no,' said Mum. 'I'd go mad.'

So we were kept a secret until on May 3 I was born, all six pounds of me, followed by George twenty minutes later and a little heavier. When the nurse brought us in to show Mum all she could think to say was : 'Don't they look funny!'

The nurse said : 'Aren't you horrible—these are going to be six-footers, you mark my words. What are you going to call them?'

Of course Mum hadn't thought about two names, but one of the other nurses made up her mind for her when she took a peep at us and said :

'They're a proper little Henry and George.'

Boxing people later came to know George as Jim, because there was another boxer called George Cooper at the time, but Mum and Dad were at once taken with Henry and George as the names were in both sides of the family. Dad was Henry William, and his father was George.

Dad and Mum were from the Elephant, the Elephant and Castle, that is, and so were their families, although when we were born they were living in Daneville Road, Camberwell Green. A lot of people get their Londoners confused. I live now in Wembley in a quiet cul-de-sac in a house I helped build myself. North-west Londoners, if you like. Come to that, so is Albina, my wife, though she was born on a farm in the foothills of the Italian Apennines. But Mum, Dad, Bern—four years older than us—George and me are South-east Londoners. Not East-enders. That's very different. If anyone called an Elephant kid an East-ender he'd as likely want to dot you one. Not that we had anything against East-enders. But they came from places like Mile End and Aldgate, the other side of the river.

When we were born Dad was on the trams. It was a pretty good job then, about three pounds a week, your uniform and a bit of security. But he was one of the unlucky ones who had two wars, and the hard times really came when he had to join up early in 1942. To the day he retired Dad never earned ten pounds a week, so it was always a struggle for Mum bringing up three growing boys. In the war years Dad was away in Burma for three and a half years, and she had to cope all that time on about £3 10s. a week, and no man in the house to turn to. Before Dad went away we kids were evacuated for a time. Then our house in Bellingham was blitzed, with Mum having a lucky escape, and afterwards, with Dad away, there were the doodlebugs, with South-east London catching it worse than any other place in the country, and Bern, George and me having some scrapes of our own.

We had gone to live at 120 Farmstead Road, on the Bellingham Council estate, in 1940, when I was six. That was home for me until I married Albina in January 1960. It surprises some people that of my fifty-five fights in fourteen years of professional boxing I fought twenty-eight, or just half, while I was living with Mum and Dad at Bellingham. I was still living there when I first won the British and Empire heavyweight titles against Brian London in 1959.

Our family meant a lot to us. The house we lived in was a four-room corner house, what they called a parlour type. We had a living-room with folding doors to separate the dining part, two bedrooms and a bathroom. We boys had the big bedroom. It was one of the first Council estates ever built. They started them in 1915 and finished them after the war, in 1918. They cost a lot to build even then, so we were told, and they were well-built, too. When the bombs came you would often see one house in a terrace just wiped out, but all the others still standing more or less untouched, or just the windows out.

South-east London, where we lived, was often the over-spill from Bermondsey and the dock area. There was a good railway line from Bellingham into Blackfriars, and a lot of people worked 'in the print', as we called it. A few of them were linotype operators, but mostly they had jobs in and around newspapers, magazines and printing. But whether they were tying up parcels or sweeping the floors, they got some good money, especially during and after the last war. We were the last people round our way to have a television aerial go up.

Our love of boxing mostly came from my father's side of the family. Dad was a useful amateur fighter in his Army days. He joined the Royal Artillery in 1919 and spent six years in the Regular Army and six on the reserve. He was a lead, centre and wheel driver on the gun teams, took part in the inspections by King George V and knew all about artillery and horses. He was in the final of two welterweight brigade championships. The trouble was they made him fight both on the same evening. He won the first, got dusted up by a professional in the other, and got a quid for his trouble.

I never knew Dad's father, Grandad George, but he was a great character round the Elephant. George and I used to love going up Grandma Bess's and hearing all the stories about him. We used to sit and listen to them in awe. Grandad died in 1926, years before I was born. He burst a blood vessel singing at a wedding. He was sixty-one at the time, but he'd been a pretty good boxer in his time. He looked after fighters, fought them himself, and boxed exhibitions as a sparring partner. Bare knuckles or gloves, it didn't matter. For six months he sparred with Ted Pritchard, the old middleweight champion. In those days they used to do the music halls, going round on the stage and doing these exhibitions. He used to know them all and take them home—boxers like Jem Mace. Once they got him as a bouncer, him and a few others, to keep Jack Johnson, the world heavyweight champion, out of the old National Sporting Club. Johnson, they said, had broken his word with them about defending his title. Really they were putting the block on him because they didn't like his way of life. He was coloured of course and he'd also upset a lot of people through marrying a white woman.

Anyway, Grandad had to ask him politely to leave and he did so without any trouble. Another time Grandad looked after Bombardier Billy Wells at the Palace down at the Elephant. They were frightened the boys would get after him, picking his pockets and that sort of thing—a right mob they must have been round there in those days. With Grandad looking after him they knew he'd be all right. Grandad was well known there, not just for his singing and his knowledge of horses, but for his fists.

In those days if any family had a row they went out and had a stand-up fight. Grandad used to fight like a man and my Gran wasn't like most women, scratching and pulling hair; she could punch like a man. She used to roll up her sleeves and stand up and box. If two families had a row my Grandad would fight the other man and my Gran would go and fight his wife. They were hard times.

Dad tells a story about one Sunday when he was ten or eleven. They were living at Salisbury Buildings, and Grandad was standing out in the alleyway. They used to have three iron posts at each end of those old alleyways and Grandad was leaning against one with his arm in a sling. He'd done something to his hand. There was a gypsy family round that way, called Beavis. The old man used to wear ear-rings and corduroys, and his wife—well, she was a proper terror. Grandma went down to get some milk and this Beavis woman said something to Grandad. And as Grandma passed, she said:

'You're a——woman.'

'No, I'm not,' said Grandma. 'I'm a——man.'

And wallop! That was it. They were really having a go. When this gypsy woman got on top my Grandad forgot about his injured arm and rolled them over.

'That's where you got to be,' he said to Grandma. 'On top.'

If Grandad got in a squabble, Grandma was with him, and vice versa.

Grandad's chief business was horses. They'd have all the gypsies and didikyes bring the horses up to the Repository, where the buying and selling would go on, and naturally there was always likely to be a free fight if it wasn't done properly. The Repository was the sale room underneath the archway opposite the Trocadero. Twice a week, Mondays and Fridays, they'd have sale days and Grandad and his brother used to ride the horses up and down showing them off. Runners-up they called them. If you stood in the middle of the Elephant and Castle these days, God help you. You'd be mown down by the cars and lorries. But then it was all horses—they brought all the food and drink into the city. Hansom cabs, even the buses, were drawn by horses. Grandad was marvellous with horses. No one could fiddle him. He used to run his hands down their flanks and tell the gypsies straight away whether they were worth buying. All along Station Road the gypsies would have these stalls—traps they called them—for the horses.

Grandad used to make plenty of money. He had another job as a furniture porter and he often carried a white apron with him. But he couldn't keep a pound in his pocket. He'd make a few quid, then it was off to the pub—Grandma wouldn't see him for a couple of days. He didn't have a penny when he died, but he used to make a load sometimes, either with the horses, singing his songs, chucking out or fighting for guineas. When he was nineteen he took twenty-two stallions to the Tsar of Russia's court in St Petersburg. The men had to sleep with the horses, they were that valuable. They went through France, Belgium, Holland and Germany, leaving some here and some there, and wound up with five at St Petersburg. Grandad said they were the first thoroughbred racing bloodstock the Russians ever had —this would be over eighty years ago. The Russians wanted British stallions to improve their breed. But Grandad couldn't go anywhere without a bit of a set-to. They did the journey by train and in Belgium there was a feller in the stable who was about as big a bully as you could meet. He was massive, according to Grandad, weighing about seventeen stone and an enormous height. He was in charge of the grooming, and when he shouted 'Break' they all had to stop what they were doing and get the horses out in teams of four and six. On one occasion Grandad went on with what he was doing and this feller came up and called him everything. But Grandad had seen he was wearing a lovely pair of boots, spring sides they called them, and he fancied them a bit. So when this bloke got awkward, he thought he'd just give him one. The big feller went down like a log. As he lay there the boots caught Grandad's eye again. 'Fitted me like a glove they did. Didn't have no more trouble with him either,' he told Dad.

After he'd had a few drinks Grandad used to go on and on with his stories. 'Drove you mad,' Dad said. 'In the end we'd all go to bed. "Don't encourage him," your Gran would say. We'd hear him talking in the kitchen still. No one there.'

Grandad wasn't a very big man, about Dad's size—five foot nine or so—but he was pretty useful with his fists. One day though, he got a bit more than he bargained for. It was at the Flying Horse, by the archway at the Elephant, and he saw this hunchback there, playing an organ. Suddenly the hunchback turned on a girl and started to belt her—people could be wicked in those days. Grandad went over thinking he'd stop it, and he's taking her part, thinking he was helping her, and suddenly she's turned round and stuck a great hat pin straight into his backside. Six or seven inches long, those pins were. I suppose it must have been the hunchback's wife. Anyway this hunchback was a bit of a wrestler and he turned on Grandad and threw him six or seven times. In the end Grandad had to get the crowd to make him stand up and fight.

Grandad was a middleweight, about 11 stone 6 in his prime, but that didn't stop him fighting heavyweights. He used to fight everywhere, but mostly in the backyards of pubs. At Denmark Hill, near Camberwell Green, there is a pub, the Fox Under the Hill, where in Grandad's day in the 1880s and 1890s they used to get a purse both for singing and boxing. One day the old man beat a chap called Big Arthur Smith at singing, then turned round and fought him. He beat him at that, too. Grandad also fought one of the famous Gutteridge twins—Reggie Gutteridge, the *Evening News* boxing writer, is a grandson. But it was easy come, easy go. Whatever they had went on booze. He'd get a few shillings and he'd be drunk maybe for days after that. Ted Pritchard used to introduce my Grandad by saying, 'Here's a man who could do better than me if he took it seriously.' I suppose stories like that sunk in with me. Grandad was also a bit of a trainer. A young Irish kid came over and they found him sitting on my Gran's doorstep. He was tall and skinny and he used to fight under the name of Puddingy Sullivan. My Grandad used to love meat puddings, so that was good enough for him. Sullivan slept and ate with them while Grandad was training him up. He won twenty-five open competitions in the old National Sporting Club and he was a hell of a good fighter, but then he left and went back to Ireland, much to Grandad's disappointment.

Grandad had a marvellous memory for songs. They would give him a pound just to write out a song, and a pound then was a lot of money. When he was getting on a bit he still used to come home from sale days with a pocketful of money. In freezing cold weather he would go there, and because he'd got arthritis in his hands he couldn't get them in his pocket. They were in a terrible state. 'See how much money I've got in my pocket,' he used to say. Dad would put his hand in and find a load of sixpences, shillings and two bobs that people had given him for singing and writing songs. Grandad's mother was Irish and he learned these songs off her. *Paddy Stole the Rope* was a good one, thirteen verses of it. This was long before television and radio and you had to make your own entertainment. *Donnelly and Cooper* was another one. It was a song of the famous knuckle fight on The Curragh. Gypsy Cooper—no relation so far as I know—represented England against the Irishman, Donnelly, and where they fought in Kildare they still have the footprints. It's called Donnelly's Hollow and when Dad was in Ireland he thought he'd just have to go and see that. In the song it all comes in. Donnelly went down twice, and part of Grandad's song went, 'Get up, get up, brave Donnelly,' which he did; he beat Cooper in the end. The fight went on and on, four hours they fought. So did Grandad's song, verses and verses of it. Dad always said they were marvellous songs, but he didn't know anyone who knew *Paddy Stole the Rope* except Grandad. It was a song about two labouring Irishmen, to London they did come. They had no money so they decided to rob a church. One climbs into the belfry and cuts the rope, and he comes down with the bell and lands on the other one. When Dad's mates had nothing to do they used to say, 'Is your Dad in? Can we come in and see him?' He could tell such marvellous tales. It was sad he died at sixty-one. He was at this wedding, singing a song, and he burst a blood vessel. Loads of blood came up, poor old chap, in the middle of this song, and he never recovered.

CHAPTER TWO

Dad inherited a lot from his father, his love of boxing, the songs and the horses. I wouldn't say they passed the love of horses on to me, but Dad was a good rider. In the Army they taught him to go over the jumps with no saddle, no bridle, no holding on. Once he came out of the Army it was all finished. They came from a poor working class area and they just couldn't afford horse-riding. People had such hard lives years ago. Mum's mother, Maria, lived just south of the river in Borough High Street. She'd have to get up at four in the morning, walk over London Bridge and be at the Bank of England at five o'clock. Then it was all scrubbing on hands and knees and raking out the fires, no fancy things to help you. She had twenty fires to rake out; my mother has seen her hands all chapped and bleeding, so cut that you would have thought someone had got a razor and slashed them. They'd have these huge marble floors to do, and she wouldn't skip anything. That's who my Mum, Lily, takes after. Grandma Maria lived in Red Cross Street later, and though she was getting on her place was like a new pin. She had to bring up her family because her mother, Mum's grandmother that would be, died when she was a girl of twelve. The father had money but he just disappeared: they could more easily in those days. The family lived in Bethnal Green, and they were so short of money and so cold that there were times when they had to break down the banisters of the staircase and burn them in the fire. But Grandma Maria survived all that and she was eighty-five when she died just after the war. We saw a lot of her during the war—we saw more of her than we did Grandma Bess. Most weekends we'd go up there and first thing we'd do was to go to the oven, and I guarantee she always had a bread pudding in there for us. She made bread pudding which was out of this world. Mum's was good, but Gran's had a taste all of its own, with great big sultanas in it, when she could get them. Mum and Gran were always poor, but whatever money they had they put together and it mostly went on food. If we wanted any clothes Gran would sometimes go to a moneylender for a few quid, and then she'd go out and do a bit of charring to pay it back. She was really good to us.

Even when the raids were on in the war George and me would try and get up to see her at weekends. Often she would be down London Bridge Underground. If she wasn't at home, that's where we would go. People used practically to live there during the night bombing, dressing and undressing in front of each other, and sleeping on blankets and mattresses on the platform. The older ones didn't like to give up their pitch. We'd see her there, then get off home before dark.

Grandma had a bad leg for years, but still she'd come down and visit us on the old 47 bus from London Bridge to Bellingham later in the war. She'd walk right along past the old sports field and her leg would be killing her. She'd grumble like hell, but she still managed to get there. When she got a bit bad she came to live with us for a while after the war, then she went back to her own place, but she died shortly afterwards. She was a good old sort. I reckon she had the hardest life of any of us.

Everything I remember really begins with our house in Farmstead Road at Bellingham. It was the sort of house Mum and Dad had longed for and that's where we grew up. As you went into the front door there was a fairly large hallway with the stairs leading up from it to two bedrooms. The kitchen was to the right, then on the left you had two rooms with partitioning doors, but we took those out later to make one big dining- and sitting-room. Upstairs the three boys shared the biggest bedroom, me and George sleeping together and Bern separately. There was also a bathroom with a toilet in it. It was a typical council estate road, all the houses more or less alike. Ours was a bit different because it was a corner house with a very big rambling garden in the front and a poky postage stamp garden behind. Next door on one side there was what used to be a railway bridge and a track running up to it. The bridge was disused and there was a grassy bank on our side which was our playground. We could kick a football on it, and there were a few trees where we could climb. We'd have boxing matches there with socks over our hands and generally lark about with the other kids. There weren't any Black

Hand gangs or Hell's Angels or anything like that. Farmstead Road was a long road, kind of L-shaped, and the kids we played with were from our end. We didn't know much about the others.

We went to Athelney Road School past the sports field towards Catford. It was a fair way—over ten minutes walk, I suppose. But it was good exercise, and we'd do it in all weathers, wind, rain and snow. You just couldn't afford a bike, not with three kids in the family, all growing up and always hungry. We could knock a pair of shoes out in a week. My Mum would buy us a new pair and then she'd go mad seeing a big hole in the sole. A new pair of trousers and, rip! you'd have a big tear in them. We'd go home and get out Mum's needlework box and put these big stitches in it, hoping she might not notice. But she'd see. And wallop! We got plenty off Mum, especially when Dad was away. She had to bring us up on her own.

Later on, when we got a bit bigger and we were sticking our elbows up and she was hurting her hand when she hit us, off would come her shoe.

I believe in a bit of that sometimes. It never made us neurotic. It's all part of growing up. Kids have to be chastised and after all, we weren't angels. Little hooligans really. My kids are angels compared with us. John Pietro is still a bit young but when I was Henry Marco's age I was a right urchin. All the same, if they get a little bit saucy they get a smack on the behind. I don't hit them round the face or head, but they get plenty of wallops on the legs. I haven't got a cane. I don't believe in that, not like we had when we were evacuated in 1940.

Everything seemed to happen that year. We had to go to Lancing, near Worthing on the Sussex coast. Then Mum and Dad were bombed out of Farmstead Road and they went to work in the West Country. There Dad had his fingers crushed in a three-ton roller and was out of work, and we were as miserable as sin.

We were only six years old in 1940 when we three boys had to leave London. I can always remember, Mum couldn't afford to get us any rucksacks like most of the other kids, so she made them by cutting up an old mac and we put all our stuff in it. So with these bundles on our backs and carrier bags for our food for the journey they took us to the station. They tried to explain to us but we didn't really know what was happening. I can remember getting to Lancing—it could have been Shanghai for all I knew—and they put George and me in one house and Bern in another. I can remember them saying to me and George, this is your house, and meeting this elderly woman and her daughter and son.

And I can remember sitting in there, all miserable, and looking out the window, crying, and them saying, 'What are you crying for?' And we couldn't give an answer. We were just crying.

I'm not going to knock the woman, because me and George were right little ruffians, but we didn't enjoy it. She was a disciplinarian, which was fair enough, but did she believe in the cane! There was a cane on the table at every meal, and children had to be seen and not heard. There were two other evacuees there, a little baby and another boy. Three of us used to sleep across the width of the bed. We went to a local school but we couldn't go on the beach because it was all mined, with barbed wire and concrete blocks. There was a load of Canadian troops, I remember. We were there for almost a year, but Mum and Dad were in Gloucestershire by then and they could only afford to come and see us once every few months. I suppose it taught us a bit of self-reliance, but we didn't appreciate it at the time. Mum used to send us sweets but they were rationed out to one a night. The old girl was a proper country-woman, and she used to make all her own jams and jelly, but she kept the jelly to herself. We used to like the straw-berry jam best but she'd say, 'You've got to have plum this week, all the strawberry's going too quick.' And that one jar used to have to last the week. Friday night was bath night and after that she would give us all a big spoonful of black treacle that was supposed to be good for our blood, or something, and make us go regularly. At the table no one talked. The daughter was a bit of a disciplinarian, too. If anyone talked without being spoken to, whack! came the cane. They had to be strict with us, I suppose.

Not long after we left home our house was blitzed. One Saturday night in one of the early night raids, two land mines dropped, one hung up in the trees and one hit the ground. Houses went down right, left and centre and twenty-five of our neighbours were killed. It was a terrific piece of luck that Mum was at her sister's because her husband worked at nights at the *News of the World*. Two of her sister's sons were in the Army and of course Saturday was a production night at the *News of the World* and she wanted some company down her Anderson shelter in the garden—they used to sleep in them if the warning had gone. It was only five minutes round the corner and suddenly they heard this terrific crash. Ronnie, Mum's sister's other boy, was out at the time—'Too daring,' his Mum used to say. He comes dashing into the shelter and says, 'Aunt Lil, do you live by the railway bridge?' We hadn't been there that long and he hadn't been to our house. Mum says, 'Yes, that's where we are.' He says, 'It's all gone. You don't live there any more. It's all burning and lots of people are killed.' Dad was on the trams at the time, working late. When they went round to see the house most of the walls were blown out or cracked and bedroom stuff was all over the garden. They couldn't imagine it as their place. The men were still getting people out of the bomb wreckage until the following Wednesday. Dad was passing when they got the last one out. They lifted up a sack and found this little cripple boy. Opposite our house there was a woman with two little children whose husband worked at Sainsbury's. She was just expecting a third. Her husband's mate, who worked on the vans, popped in just to pass on a message from the husband that he was working late. The mines dropped just as he called and the lot of them were killed. We had an Anderson shelter in our garden, and if Mum had been in it she might have been all right, though the blast tipped it over.

They told Dad it was going to be a long job repairing the house, and he could believe it. One day he passed by as the repair gang were going over it and there was one fellow playing a mouth organ—my mouth organ he'd pulled out of one of the drawers. Gave the repair mob a fit, Dad did, turning up like that.

Dad's driving mate had a relation in Gloucestershire, so they decided they would evacuate there, Mum by train, and Dad on the back of a motor bike. Freezing cold he says it was. He couldn't walk when he got off. Dad got a job at an asbestos factory and Mum at an aircraft factory, making bomb racks for Lancasters. Then Dad had his accident, crushing three fingers in the three-ton roller. He was out of work for a year and all he got was £2 a week sick pay. Mum and Dad were living in an old cottage which had been condemned, but they had opened it up for them, charging half-a-crown a week rent.

Finally Dad got £200 compensation and straightaway they shut up the cottage, came down to Lancing to pick us up, rigged us out with some new clothes in Brighton, and eventually we went back to London. Dad went to Catford Town Hall and they said, 'Where have you been? We've been looking for you.' He found out why all too soon. They gave him £40 compensation! Most of our furniture and bits had been destroyed or nicked. A neighbour got £300 and according to Dad their house was scarcely touched, but Mum and Dad had gone away and that was it. While we were waiting for our old house to be repaired—it took eighteen months all told—they moved us into a flat in Grove Park. They were private flats that had been requisitioned, and it was our first taste of luxury living. In the bathroom we had a shower attachment and I can remember saying, 'Cor, we're posh, we've got a shower in our bathroom.' We finally moved back into Farmstead Road, but we had quite a few wartime adventures to come.

Later on, when the doodlebugs came and we were right in their alley, we had the ceilings or bits of them down two or three times. We had a radiogram which was Dad's pride and joy. But one day the windows were blown in and there were bits of glass stuck all over the top of it, like one of those walls to keep the burglars out. Pat, our wire-haired terrier, had a bit of whippet in her. Every time she thought she heard the bombs coming she'd whip inside Dad's radiogram—all the works were in the top and there was just room for her to curl up. With these bits of glass in the top it was a proper little fox-hole. We still used to play the thing, of course. George was a good polisher, and he kept at this glass until in the end you could hardly see it.

The chief war danger often came from our own side. There were all these anti-aircraft guns up Beckenham way, and all the shrapnel would patter down like rain. If a doodlebug was coming really close Mum would shout, 'Quick!' and she made us grab a cushion each and rush to shelter holding the cushions over our heads. You can just imagine the Cooper kids galloping about like that. I don't know what good a cushion would have done against a piece of falling shrapnel, but Mum had her ideas and it didn't do to stop and argue. Once those doodlebug engines cut out everyone learned to dive for the shelter. One Saturday night Bern and me were going round selling the weekly 'highest score' football tickets up Southend Lane. We could see this V1 coming near and we just dashed towards the nearest Anderson shelter. You only had a little square hole to get through, and while I'm getting in, Boof! The blast blew me straight against the side of the shelter and knocked me cold. Bern was behind me and when I came to he was picking the glass bits out of his backside. We laughed. Somehow as kids you didn't see any danger. Bombs, explosions and I suppose death were commonplace. A bomb or a doodlebug would drop and you'd be round with a load of kids to see the damage. 'Cor, fancy three dead in there,' one kid said to me once. Next week he was dead. The day we heard Lewisham Woolworths had caught it with a V2 rocket we ran all the way there, about three miles. It was one of the worst tragedies of the war. They were bringing out bits of bodies, and as one of the rescue workers came out with a carrier bag we were told he had a head in it. We'd go back and play afterwards. You knew it could happen to you but it didn't keep you awake at nights, it didn't seem to penetrate. I suppose we were too young to have any deep feelings about it.

At the same time there are impressions you pick up as a kid which you know will last the rest of your life. I have always had a good sense of smell. The smell of a British boxing ring is altogether different from a Continental one. I was lucky that I never had any serious injury to my nose. I was always able to breathe well through the nose when I was boxing, and a lot of my earliest memories are to do with the smells as well as the sights of South-east London. You still had lots of horses being used by tradesmen in those days. Kids today don't get those horsey smells. Horses drew the milk and the bread floats, and you'd have them watering and doing their business in the streets outside your door. You'd have a few tomato plants in your back garden so you'd have to go out and shovel up the manure. Smartish, too, or someone would beat you to it. When we were evacuated that was our job on Saturday mornings—scouring the streets for manure for her tomato plants with a barrow and a couple of buckets.

Price's, the bread people, always had horses and carts. Then you had the old winkle man who used to come round on Sundays. A right old gravelly voice he was. He had the sorest throat in London. 'Wink-olls. . . .' Nat Gonella, the trumpet player, was his brother. He used to come around on an old three-wheel bike with a box on the front. That was a marvellous tea, your celery and your winkles—the traditional Londoner's Sunday tea. I still love seafood. I haven't had any winkles for years, but I love oysters—I've matured to the more expensive things! Then there were the rag and bone men with their special cries. Kids nowadays don't hear these things round the streets. I remember the muffin man with his bell and the flat tray of crumpets on his head, and of course the sweep. Everyone was burning coal then and the sweep was a common sight with his old brushes, and black as the ace of spades. As kids you'd all have a go at him, and he'd chase you. Then someone would kick his bag over and make a right old mess. There were the knifegrinders, carpet binders, chair repairers, and you'd see a guy sitting on the kerb repairing all the frayed coconut mats. I've sometimes wondered where they all went to, how they finished up.

Life became really hard for us when Dad was called up in March 1942 at the age of 40. He'd been in the artillery and knew all about guns, so they put him in the Medical Corps. He never did fathom why. Dad was sent up to Edinburgh Castle, then he was off to the Far East and we didn't see him for nearly four years. His own pay as a private was twenty-one shillings and with allowances Mum had £3 10s. out of which she had to find a guinea a week rent. Mum went as skinny as a rake with the worry of it. Sometimes she went to the Soldiers, Sailors and Air Force Families Association for help, she was working herself as well as looking after us, and of course we kids had to set to and make what few shillings we could.

Mum did a bit of charring, she worked in a laundry, and then she got a job in the school canteen. The only time Dad had ten results up on his football pools we forgot to post the coupon. Ten results, all correct, and there was his letter sitting on the mantelpiece! Some people during the war never seemed to be short of anything, but nothing fell off a lorry for us. We just had the bare rations and that was it. Mum often waited in a long queue at the grocers, then just as she got to the counter they'd say, 'Sorry, all gone, that's it.' Mum never had time to sit down and read us stories. There was always something you had to do. You'd be off to the gasworks to get some coke or coal bits, or you'd be at the Red Cross getting a parcel – I will always remember the gaudy American shirts you sometimes had to wear. In the war you had to queue for everything, and Saturday mornings Mum would get all three boys organised. At Catford there was a shop called Kennedy's which sold good sausages, and the queue used to form at half-past seven in the morning. The shop opened at nine o'clock, so one of us would take it in turns to get in the queue early so that when Mum had done the rest of the shopping she would come and take our place. Another of us would have to get the bread, another would wait in the margarine queue. Getting the coke was one of the big jobs because you'd have to fill up your sack then lug it from Sydenham to Bellingham, nearly three miles and uphill all the way.

Nothing was ever wasted. Bread pudding, suet pudding, date pudding, shinbone soups—these were the sort of things Mum reckoned would fill us up. Her bread pudding was my favourite. I could tell anyone the recipe now. Stale bread soaked in water, then the water squeezed out. Afterwards flour, raisins, spice, beef dripping, and two or three eggs mixed in, then baked. The smell was lovely. You couldn't get dried fruit except at Christmas at one period of the war. That was awful. If we heard one shop had pressed dates we'd go diving off down there, but often we were disappointed.

Of course we loved jam, but the ration was one pound a month, and we could get through our four pounds in a week. Once Mum thought she'd got the answer with some guava jam—God knows where it came from, but even we couldn't face that. It stuck in its tin in the larder for about six months before we threw it away. To pay for our clothes Mum sometimes had a Co-op cheque. You could get a cheque, say for a pound, and then pay it back interest free at a shilling a week. She liked to get an identical sports coat and trousers for George and me, but of course the Co-op would fit one of us up then find they hadn't the size to match it. So we'd get sore feet making a round of all the Co-ops up to New Cross trying to get a match. I suppose people got to know us a bit even then. Not long ago I was at a do sponsored by Bovril when a fellow came up and said, 'I don't suppose you remember me, Henry?' I looked at him hard, and then my memory clicked. 'Oh, yes, I do. I can't remember your name, but you were on the fats counter of Bellingham Co-op, twenty-five years ago.' So he was. He'd left the Co-op and started his own grocery business, but I spent so long in the margarine and lard queue I knew every hair on his head, and though he'd lost a few since then I still knew him.

As time went on we did all sorts of jobs to help Mum out. When we were quite small we would get half-a-crown from the milkmen for helping push their three-wheeler carts on a Saturday morning. As we got a bit older we took paper rounds, earning 7s. 6d. a week which we gave to Mum to help run the home. At first we had no bike, there were flats everywhere, and the strap used to cut your shoulder in half by the time you'd walked the three or four miles of the round. Dumfield Flats up Southend Lane were absolute murder from the bottom to the top. By the time you got home, had a quick cup of tea and set off for school you were like a dished out rag. Bern was the envy of most of his pals. He had a really good job at Newman's in Bellingham, getting a pound a week when he was still a schoolboy of fifteen. The fellow must have liked him. George and me worked at the same paper shop. We had to be up at six and down at the shop by six-thirty. Not like kids nowadays, we had big boards with the names and addresses and had to mark all our own papers. The old guy would open up the door at six-thirty, and we'd have to lug all the bundles of papers inside, and do all the sorting out ourselves. Then we'd have to go out and deliver them. The last paper of the main round was at a house about half a mile away from all the others. When you've done that for six days a week you've had it for the seventh and sometimes I used to sling the paper in the hedge. Then the old fellow would get on the 'phone to the guvnor and say : 'Where's my paper?' And I'd say : 'Someone must have nicked it or something. Sorry.'

We had some great ways for making a bob or two. Up at Beckenham Park there was Beckenham Golf Course. A lot of holes go through the woods, and we would wait until they teed off, then nip out of the trees, nick the ball off the fairway, and run round in a big circle back to the clubhouse. We'd sell it there to another golfer for two bob or half-a-crown because golf balls in the war years were scarce. Other times we'd say: 'Can we help you find your ball, mate?' Then if we found it he'd give you a tanner. One day just after we'd started doing this we were looking for about ten minutes to a quarter of an hour without finding it. Just as we were giving up, I spotted it and shouted: 'Here it is!' The golfer was very grateful and gave me a tanner. When he'd gone, Bern gave me a dig in the back: 'You're a right nit. I'd seen that ages ago. We could have sold that up the clubhouse for half-a-crown.' Then we'd go round to the greengrocers getting old boxes, chopping them up for firewood, and selling it at sixpence a bundle. It wasn't all work, of course. We would have our seasons—conkers, pre-war fag cards, where you'd lean them against a wall and flick them down, skates (not that Mum could afford any for us), marbles, carts and scooters made with ballbearing wheels. The noise up and down the streets was something awful when the scooters were in.

At school the Cooper twins always stuck out like a sore thumb. We were a bit on the big side, and other kids would say when asked about some trouble: 'Well, I don't know who they were but I know the Cooper twins were there.' So we would be hauled up in front of the headmaster, Mr Davies, and he'd listen to our story and say: 'One thing I like about you Coopers, you always tell the truth.' But that never stopped him fiddling in the back of his cupboard and bringing out his cane. I guarantee the name Cooper was top of the list in the cane book. If I had the cane three times a week I thought I was getting off lightly. It was always on the hands, and off the headmaster I didn't mind the cane. He had a short, thick old cane and he never really hurt you. We had another teacher, the maths master, and he was different altogether. He made you stand with your hand well out, and he'd judge and time it so that he caught just the tips of your fingers. Boy, you felt that for an hour or two afterwards! I used to turn my head away and flinch when it was coming. One day I overdid it, and as he came over with the cane I pulled my hand away just enough for him to miss. Not just miss but go right through to whack his own leg. Oh, blimey! It was the worst thing I could have done. I got another two for that.

I didn't like school. We had a woman teacher who took history, and I loved that, and still do, because she made it so interesting. If you like a person I think you'll learn. She got us to act things, and I liked that too. But with teachers I didn't like I'm afraid I put up a barrier and wouldn't learn, just to spite them I suppose. But they were usually the people trying to drum it in. I wasn't a great scholar and I would be the first to admit it. Fractions, algebra and geometry I couldn't do then, let alone now. I pity Henry Marco when he's doing his homework. Once he passed the ten-year old standard he lost me : he was on his own. Yet I can look after my household and business things, and in the professional boxing game you've got to be able to work out your figures quick, though of course in Jim Wicks, my manager, I had a marvellous man for that.

I was never one for fiction. I never bothered with *Wizard* and *Champion* and that sort of comic with stories. Westerns and detective stories leave me cold. I recently read *Rise and Fall of the Third Reich*, by William Shirer, and that's the sort of book I like. Encyclopædias, history, true-life adventures, instructional books, these are the things that appeal to me.

In the school playground I probably learned as much as I did in the school itself. We were lucky, George and me, that being the pair of us and both big for our age we were never bullied. The first fight I ever had was a complete accident really, with a boy called Orwood who afterwards became quite a friend, because we went into senior boxing at the same time and his brother became a professional and sparred with us. I couldn't have been more than seven when it happened. He wouldn't give us back our ball and so we had a fight, if you could call it that. In fact we just shaped up to each other for ten minutes, all threatening like, and after a while I was saying to myself : 'What have I started here?' Then when we did get to grips it was only to wrestle; I think most playground fights are like that. The first serious set-to was much later. There was a little clique in the school and one day me, George and one or two others were playing against them at handball. The referee was one of their chums. Everything they did was OK; everything we did was penalised. So, in the end, we decided if they wanted to play it that way so would we, and we began to get a bit rough with them, barging in and grabbing the ball. Suddenly a little fellow called Bridges comes and jumps on my back and starts throwing punches. I get a bit of a temper up and drag him over me and punch him in the eye. He's lying there knocked out. Another fellow rushes over but George holds him off. Little do we know but the school nurse it crossing the playground just at this moment. She's crying and upset. There's Bridges lying on the deck with a great big fat eye. He's out. She says between sobs : 'To think that such big boys are going on like this when there's so much fighting in the world. You could be doing good instead of fighting.' Oh dear, there was uproar. The teachers had us all up and the Coopers' name went into the cane book again.

We had a few special friends at the school and in Bellingham, and there are two in particular, Johnny Gibson and Jimmy Rushton, we still see regularly. They went boxing at the same time as we did, and both were among the few people in our dressing-room even up to the last fight with Joe Bugner. Johnny lives up in Bedfordshire and has a good business fixing windscreens for cars which break them on the M1. Jimmy is a sheet metal worker, a year or two younger than us, but we first knew him on the estate. Both were at the party of about twenty close friends and relatives who came back home to Wembley for a few drinks after my last fight, against Joe Bugner. After all our London fights we'd reckon to have a few people back, and they would be there if they could make it.

CHAPTER THREE

George and me were always very close. The only time we parted was when I got married. Even then, with Dad retired and him and Mum going to live at Margate, George came to live here at Wembley until he was married. We went to school together, we went boxing together, we were together in the Army. We look alike, we think alike, in temperament we're similar, and often we catch ourselves repeating each other's remarks. We like the same things. We used to go to the cinema two or three times a week; every weekend for years we went to see a film in the West End. We never argued which film to see; one would say, 'Let's go and see that,' and the other would straightaway agree. We had the same tastes so that even when it was a bad film we could agree about that. George will say something and he's just beaten me to it. I'm about to say exactly the same thing. We don't feel each other's pain, or anything like that; even in identical twins I think that's very rare. Throughout our boxing lives I would go on first so that I wouldn't be worrying over George's fight when I got into the ring. But otherwise it's little things. I might say, 'Let's have a ride over to see Uncle Jim tomorrow,' and George would say, 'Cor, I was just going to say that.' Bern, my eldest brother, was slimmer and slighter than either of us, and preferred athletics and football to boxing. He always followed us, like Dad and Mum's brother, Tom Nutkins, seeing all the fights he could—Dad wouldn't miss one of our fights in England.

George was a better cricketer than I was; at school he was a better batsman. I'd look good until the ball came, and then I'd have a slash and get out. I was a left-hander and George played right. At soccer I always played in goal, and I think I could have done something if I had kept at it. I played for my district, the Borough of Lewisham, as a fourteen-year-old junior, but when we took up boxing seriously we had to drop the other sports for fear of injury. George was a half back or back, being a bit on the tall side. We kept playing football for a while after our school days, and at one time we both played for the gasworks where we had a job. We had a bash at athletics as schoolboys, but I was never all that good. We dabbled at rowing for one season. The secretary of our boxing club at that time was a member of the Globe Rowing Club, near Greenwich, and we went down there regularly one summer when the winter boxing season was finished. Of a Sunday morning we'd get the boat out at Greenwich and row right up to Tower Bridge in a coxed four. I used to love that. It's a pity, but when you dedicate yourself to one sport, such as boxing, you can't start developing your muscles in a different sort of way in another sport.

I am totally left-handed. I do everything with my left hand rather than my right. The only thing I was never inclined to do left-handed was box in the orthodox left-hander's way. Most left-handed people are southpaws, that is they lead with the right hand and hold their left hand defensively, covering up their body and their jaw as best they can, until they want to land a really heavy blow, when they let their stronger left hand go. I bowled and batted left-handed at cricket, I write left-handed, I play golf left-handed and I even shoot with the butt on my left shoulder. All the power was in the left. It was something I took for granted until in boxing I discovered just how to use it. But even then, the left hook, or 'Enery's 'Ammer' as Jim Wicks christened it, didn't come all at once. I started boxing in the orthodox way, leading with my left, and I soon discovered I had a very good straight left punch. But in the early days I didn't have such a marvellous left hook. George used to stop more boys than I did with his right hand—he had a hell of a good right-hand punch, George did, but I always had a good left jab. I'd jab them silly. The referee would stop a fight because a boy would have his face bleeding from the belting I would be giving him with this jab, jab. Over the years, people training me or massaging me all noticed how developed I was on the left side rather than the right. It's a bit like Rod Laver's racket arm, which they say is half as thick again as his other arm. In theory you might argue that if you worked for three years on the other arm you could develop equal power. But it doesn't operate like that. Power of that sort develops over a lifetime. When I was a kid not long left school, plastering developed my left arm a lot. In those days you pushed sand and cement about. These days the mortar mix is as light as a feather, but, then, pushing sand and cement against a wall or up on to a ceiling really developed your muscles. I had injuries to my left hand over the years, and doctors told me when I was X-rayed at the age of twenty-six that it had the wear of a man of seventy years of age.

I did a lot of heavy work as a youngster. Once when I had a job on a building site I was carrying a big heavy chimney cowl on a bike. Suddenly the wind caught it and blew me off, and I went down on my elbow and chipped a piece out of the bone. I went to the hospital but they had a waiting list and they told me to come back in three or four months' time. Well, I just had it bandaged up, it seemed to heal on its own and I didn't bother about going back. During my boxing career I began to have trouble with it, and when they X-rayed it they could see where there had been chips of bone. I had used the elbow so much I had slowly powdered them away and they had dispersed into the bloodstream. But it was like having grit in a joint, and that's why I had such unusual wear. They also said this left arm would pack up before anything else, but it never did, not to the point where it was impossible to go on. They always expected trouble from it and they thought that if anything stopped me it wouldn't be cut eyes but this left arm. In fact, with timing and confidence, it got better and better, and I was really at my peak when I was about twenty-five to twenty-eight in the middle years—heavyweights don't mature until they have been at it a few years. In the last two or three years of my career the arm gave us some problems, including the one disagreement between myself and Jim Wicks whether we went on with a major fight, but as boys playing with socks over our fists outside our homes in Bellingham, that was a long way over the horizon.

Dad came back from the war in 1945. It was one of the great moments of our lives. He wore one of those 14th Army hats with the side turned up, like the Australians, and he brought us lots of presents, including football boots. It also brought one of the funniest incidents of our young days, though not perhaps for George. We played a game in the school playground which could occasionally get a bit rough. Two teams would play it, each trying to capture another kid and put him in the corner until he was rescued. One of his own team would have to come in and touch him. Now Dad had cabled us saying he would be home on a certain day. On the day before we were playing this game in the playground and they've caught me and I'm in the box. George comes charging in to get me, and, of course, being a big kid, the other team see him coming and move out of the way. George goes bosh! straight through thin air and hits his head on a drainpipe. He lies on the ground for a while and we stop the game. Eventually he gets up, apparently all right, but in fact he's got concussion. We don't know that. As far as we can see he's just got a big lump and a cut on his head. We're at home, later on, when Bern says, 'Good, Dad's coming home tomorrow.' George looks at him blankly and says, 'Is he?' We'd been talking about this for three or four days, and Bern and me look at each other. Is he joking? A few minutes later we say it again, 'Dad's coming home tomorrow.' George gets all excited again. 'Is he? When? What time?' It was then that we tumbled to the fact that he'd got concussion and couldn't remember. But being kids we couldn't let him alone. We asked him all sorts of questions. 'D'you remember so and so?' He didn't know anything. Mum was dead worried. She got dressed and took him down to the doctor's, who told her not to worry too much. Put him to bed, give him a warm drink, let me know if he's not better tomorrow, he said. In the morning Bern and me wake to test him out before it's even light.

'Dad's coming home today.'

'Yeah, I know,' says George. His memory was back, to our disappointment. He was never concussed like that in all his boxing career.

I was nine years old—it was just after Dad had got back —when I suffered my first knock-out. George and me were sparring about in the kitchen. I went to dodge a punch and forgot how close the gas stove was. I went backwards and bang! Next I knew they were picking me up off the kitchen floor asking if I'm all right. KO'd by a gas stove! It would have made a much better story later on, but I don't know how Jim Wicks or Harry Levene would have taken it. In all my boxing career I was never concussed in the way George was that time. In fifty-five pro fights I was knocked clean out three times—by Ingemar Johansson, Floyd Patterson and Zora Folley. Directly I came to, my faculties were there straightaway. The good punches you never see coming. You feel no pain at all. It's like being in a room with the lights on and someone coming in and turning them off and it's pitch black. All you remember is coming to, just waking up. There's no pain, no soreness with a really good knockout blow. It's as if someone had just turned the lights on again. You get a similar sensation when they

32

give you pentathol in hospital. One, two, three and you're out, just like a knock-out. It happened to me twice later on, first when I went for neck manipulation, then for a cartilage operation.

I suppose everything was beginning to add up to a boxing career, though I would never have guessed it as a nine year old. There wasn't a lot of religion in our life, but we always went to Sunday School, and we were always in the church plays at Christmas. I was never top of the bill—a King or one of the Wise Men or something—but I used to love it. There's a bit of the actor in me. Mum never went to church, but we would go along to St Dunstan's on Bellingham of a Sunday afternoon. Most of us local kids went, just to get out from under their feet, I reckon. I was in the church Cubs, and we'd go to church parade on Sunday mornings marching behind the big Scouts and the band. We couldn't afford a uniform and all we had were those little green tabs sticking out of our socks, but that didn't matter. We'd swing our arms and stick our chests out. All fighters, basically, are show-offs, and marching with the band, bugles blowing, was just up our street. We obviously showed off a bit too much at times, especially in games like British Bulldog, where you have to dash from end to end of the hall and anyone caught has to join those in the middle in trying to capture someone and lift him off the ground. Again, George and me used to get a bit enthusiastic, and eventually we were politely asked to leave the Cubs.

It was a neighbour, Bob Hill, a local fireman who'd boxed for the Fire Brigade, who you might say discovered us as boxers. George and me were always sparring about at home, and when Dad came home from the war he would often get on his knees on the floor and box with us. Then we would go out on the grass verge with some of the local kids and organise our own matches with socks rolled round our fists. One day Mr Hill—everyone was always Mr this or Mr that to us—was watching us through his kitchen window and he made up his mind to ask Dad and Mum if he could take us to the local boxing club. 'I've been watching the two lads,' he said to Dad. 'One of them's pretty handy, in fact both of them are. Would you let them come over to Bellingham Boxing Club?' The club held regular nights at the British Legion Club's hall. Dad was quite pleased, because he was always interested in boxing. He believed it kept boys fit and got something out of the system so that none of them would want to go around beating each other up. Mum didn't worry too much at the time because it was amateur boxing and she reckoned there would be people to look after us well. All she asked was that we didn't fight each other.

It was George and me who got upset, not because of the idea of joining a club but because at first Mr Hill said he could only take one of us. That was murder. In the end they were able to take the two, and Mr Hill paid the half-a-crown a year for both of us. We were nine years old at the time. Of course we lost touch with Mr Hill when he moved away not long after the war, but a girl reporter from the *Kentish Times*, the daughter of my mother's insurance agent in Margate, managed to track him down in 1971, over twenty-five years later. All sorts of people had claimed to be related to this Mr Hill, and Dad was a bit doubtful when she said she had found him, but it proved to be the same one. He had a smallholding in the Maidstone area, and at the age of seventy-six he came on as one of the big surprises in the *This is Your Life* television programme. It was nice to be able to thank him after all those years.

Mum didn't put anything in the way of our boxing then or later, though like Albina she never wanted to watch it. When the fights were on the radio she would have it on, but she wouldn't have her ear glued to it. She'd just pop in and ask whoever was in the room, 'How's he getting on, then?' She knew enough about modern boxing to know that you don't get punchy with all the strict match-making rules there are, but she was always a bit afraid of damage. At the back of her mind, too, was the memory of the French-Canadian boxer, Del Fontaine, who they watched go from a fine, handsome young man to a murderer, hanged for shooting his girl friend, in the space of two years. This was in the middle 1930s, when we were only just born, but Fontaine and his girl friend were a marvellous looking pair around Camberwell Green. 'Arm in arm you always saw them. They looked a picture,' Mum used to say. He was good, too—he fought Tommy Farr in his time. But the girl was supposed to have jilted him, and next he was down on his heels, punchy, and no one wanting him. Of course even then lots of boxers had good careers and finished with a reasonable bit of cash, but it was the sort of experience, because it was so close to her, that made Mum just that little bit wary about boxing.

Our main trainer for our first few years was old Matt Wells, who had been British lightweight champion. He gave us the rudiments of boxing, and after that, when we were fifteen, we went to the Eltham and District Amateur Boxing Club, and there we really started to improve and make a name for ourselves. George Page was the trainer there, and he looked after and coached us until after we turned professional when we came out of the Army. What we had he brought out. George had been a very useful fighter. He fought welter, middle and light-heavyweight against top amateurs. He worked as a moulder in an iron foundry, but he really devoted himself to bringing on young amateur boxers. The most important thing he taught us was a set training routine. The discipline of that lasted throughout our boxing lives. We'd go over to him two or three times a week and on Sunday mornings, and he would get into the ring and spar with us. He would concentrate on my left hand. I would be in there for maybe half-an-hour, just throwing left hands at him. I had to keep on, bop, bop, bop. . . .

In 1952, when I was seventeen, I won my first Amateur Boxing Association championship. It may have seemed young to people who had never heard of me before, but in fact it followed years of time and effort. Though we first put on boxing gloves at Bellingham when we weren't quite ten, we didn't have a proper fight for two years. You learned simply by copying the older boys, getting the atmosphere of the gymnasium, and learning how to train. You have to learn how to skip properly. At first you only hop. Then the trainer teaches you how to hop on alternate legs. Skipping is good for timing, wind and leg muscles. It gets your hands, trunk and legs moving in synchronisation. It's an important part of your training routine to the day you retire. Sometimes I would skip for a quarter of an hour without a rest, but usually we would break it up into rounds. Three minutes of skipping straight off, then half a minute's rest, another three minutes, and so on. You combine that with bag work and shadow boxing. Bag work is not simply hitting a bag. The heavy bag you must imagine as your opponent. Each time you hit it you are picking your spot, imagining where the jaw and the solar plexus would be. On some bags they'll draw the man on it. You have to imagine as far as possible it is a man in front of you, and box him as a man. The speed ball, the ball suspended from a platform, is to get co-ordination between hand and eye. It's speed and rhythm. Always you work to three-minute periods. In pro boxing sometimes you are in training for six rounds of three minutes, at others say twelve rounds, and for a title fight, fifteen rounds. You adjust your training accordingly. The fitter you feel and the better you get so you cut your rest period down. Often we would have only half a minute's rest instead of the minute that you get in the ring. If you've done ten rounds of training and come out of it feeling fit with only half a minute's break between rounds then you feel confident of your condition for the fight, when you get twice as much rest.

The form of training has been handed down by tradition, and basically it remains the same as when Tommy Farr was fighting in the 1930s, but it has got a lot harder and faster. We've developed a few more exercises and brought weight-training into it more. Not heavy weights, because they would develop muscles where you didn't want them. Boxing training methods evolve gradually. You rarely have revolutionary things introduced. Years ago things were different in that men fought to get fit; now we have to get fit to fight. In the old days they fought two or three times a week; nowadays it's weeks or months between fights. In 1965 I fought four fights, in 1966 four, in 1967 three, 1968 one, 1969 one, 1970 two, and 1971, one, my last. Of course injury can come into it, but this gives an idea of the modern pattern. In the old days it was nothing for a fighter to end up with three or four hundred fights. It's partly the tax and the money situation—you can't afford to fight too often—but basically it's numbers. There just aren't the boxers around. Just before and after the war there were three to four thousand boxers registered with the Board of Control. Now it's more like three to four hundred. The Services encouraged boxing during the war and up to the end of National Service. The Army started a lot of boys in their careers. They stopped a lot too—they were the worst over-matchers in the world! A PTI would say, 'You and you,

you're about the same height and weight. Get in and have a round.' One kid hadn't had a round of boxing in his life, the other kid was pretty experienced, and the rookie would get a belting and say 'To hell with that, I'm not doing that any more.' It put a lot of them off, whether they were likely to be useful or not. But many did start that way, or the Services at least gave them an interest in boxing.

A lot of people are worried by the idea of pain, of getting hurt. I was myself. But being in the ring when you're warm is not like sitting and watching when you're cold and seeing a punch and thinking, 'Cor, that hurt.' When you are concentrating and active you don't feel pain. George and me both lost our first four fights as amateurs. Mum would say, 'Now you can't go and box on an empty stomach,' and she'd make a bread pudding specially. Of course the one thing a boxer can and must do is fight on an empty stomach ! So off we went, full of bread pudding, and after a round or two we would be out of breath and a kid would hit us in the stomach and we'd gasp and wince. It was agony. I thought, 'I'm not going to do this any more.' After those four fights I never thought I was going to take up boxing seriously. When someone hit me in the stomach I felt like being sick. If I went to a tournament and they said, 'We haven't got a fight for you, Cooper,' I used to say to myself, 'Lovely, now I can sit and watch the boxing.' Then if you were sitting there enjoying yourself and a voice in your ear suddenly said, 'Cooper, we've found you an opponent,' your old heart would miss a beat, and your stomach would sink into your boots. You didn't want to say, 'No, I don't want it' and make yourself look a Charlie, so you were all on edge and nervous again. But it would all disappear the moment the bell went and you really were in there fighting.

CHAPTER FOUR

We just missed leaving school at fourteen. We were choked, because we wanted to leave, but instead they brought it in that we had to stay until fifteen. We didn't leave school saying, 'I want to be a tradesman', or 'I want to be a solicitor'. We just left looking for how much an hour we

37

could get. Which was going to be the best paid job? The very first job we went to was at Burnham's in Sydenham, labouring 'on the dock', as they called it. For ninepence an hour we unloaded and stacked sheets of metal as the lorries brought them in. We had thousands of cuts on our hands.

Then I found out we could get 9½d. an hour at the Sydenham Gas Works so we left Burnham's. Then I heard there was a building firm just across the Bromley Road on Bellingham that was paying 10½d. an hour. So we went there, but they had a system where they held on to your first week's money so you worked a fortnight before you got your pay packet. When I got it I looked at the pay slip and saw they were only paying me 10d. an hour.

'Here, you've made a mistake,' I said. 'You told me 10½d.'

'Oh, no,' the fellow said, 'You've got it wrong.'

'No, I haven't. Else I wouldn't have left the other firm.'

'That's all you get,' he said.

'All right, give me my cards,' I told him.

So we left, just like that, because we weren't getting our ha'penny an hour. A matter of principle, we reckoned. Then we went into the building trade again, and stayed in it. We met a plastering contractor called Reg Reynolds—we were still only sixteen—and with him we learned the plastering trade. He was a friend of Georgie Page's at the Eltham and District Amateur Boxing Club. It was hard but skilled work and Reg was a good boss, and apart from our time in the Army it stayed our basic trade until we turned professional.

When Albina and me moved into our house in Ledway Drive, Wembley, after we were married in 1960, it was basically only a three-bedroomed place and we soon needed a bit more room. I had a 22ft by 11ft lounge built on and a bedroom overhead. George helped me, but otherwise I did all the plastering and interior decorating myself. I also did a lot of the foundation digging and overseeing. It's not just the money you save, although that matters. If you get a plasterer along he won't necessarily be a very good one, and I know that if I do it myself it'll be done properly and I'll save the money as well. I was a bit slower than I was at one time, but it wasn't too bad a job.

By the time I was sixteen, then, I was getting some good instruction in both my trades, plastering and boxing. But nothing came easy for any of the family. There were neighbours a bit later on who got a little bit envious of us. There are always people like that. When our television aerial went up I guarantee it was the last in the road. Then we bought a car, an old Ford Prefect, and we built a garage on the side of the house. There were people who had a bit to say about that, but most of them were comfortably off compared with us in the war years and for a good time afterwards. Dad used to say : 'They've got nothing to beat.' The coat Dad wore all week I used to wear for best on Sundays, and not many had to do that. But still you made your friends, and lasting friends, too. There were five of us who did every-thing together—Johnny Gibson and Jimmy Rushton of course, Don Simons and the two of us. We were known as the Five Musketeers on Bellingham. We went to the same school, went to the same boxing club, Eltham, and always together. George and me would do eight hours on the build-ing probably an hour's bus ride away. We would rush home, wash, change, Mum would have dinner ready sharp at six, up again and off. Three times a week for training, once more for the tournament. Eltham was an hour-and-a-half away on the bus—every bus driver in that part of South-east London knew us. Mum would sometimes say, 'Don't go tonight. Look, there's all that snow and ice.' But we'd say, 'Mum, do you mind. We know what we're doing.' We were that keen. If they'd tried to stop us boxing at Eltham we would have gone behind their backs.

It gave us a lot of pleasure when we started to win a few prizes. The first thing I ever won was a medal at the age of ten. The first cup was Mum's pride and joy, two and a half inches high, an inch across, and she put it on the side-board, nothing else around it, and cleaned it every day. It wasn't any bigger than an egg cup—Dad said he couldn't get drunk on the champagne in that. But I couldn't get home quick enough with it. Usually me and George would stay and see all the fights, but that night we rushed into the changing-room, got dressed, and tore home : 'Look, Mum, we've won a cup!' I reckon we won twenty canteens of cutlery before we were eighteen. Every Christmas we used to lay out the prizes and Dad's sister would come in and choose things for members of the family. 'Tommy would like this, Emma would like that.' Cake dishes, coffee per-colators, all the things on different trays. Mum's special favourites were an hors d'oeuvres dish, shaped like a ship's wheel, and a silver butter dish. Dad's love was a pair of nutcrackers which he reckoned to bring out every Christmas. 'Crack any nut there is except a coconut,' he'd say.

In eighty-four amateur bouts I won seventy-three and lost eleven. I won two Amateur Boxing Association light-heavyweight titles, fought in the Olympic Games of Helsinki in 1952 — a vintage boxing Olympics, though not for me — and in various amateur internationals. For a part of the time I was in the Army, in the famous Boxers' Battalion of that period, and it was a wonderfully enjoyable part of my life and boxing experience.

We were told in amateur boxing that if you had a good left hand and speed, those were the two main things, and you would go a long way. My strength was a left hand, and as I never liked taking punches I was glad to develop that style. Most of my wins were on points. In junior bouts you fight three two-minute rounds, but by the time you are seventeen it's three rounds at three minutes each, and sometimes four rounds. An amateur is not just a man who has never competed for money. He must not have fought for a bet, competed against any professional, or received money or made any kind of a living at any other sport. In amateur boxing there is a referee in the ring, and three judges and a timekeeper outside it. Only the judges score, and generally speaking it's the boxer who strikes his opponent more often and more cleanly who gets the maximum number of twenty points at the end of each round. The other man will get a proportion of this, depending on how many punches he has landed. If the scores are equal the winner will be the boxer who has done most leading off, which means striking first. If they are equal in that, the boxer with the better defence wins.

Boxing is in many ways a very simple, natural game. The rules are much the same as when they were drawn up by the Marquess of Queensberry and John Graham Chambers in the 1860s. You've got to hit with the knuckle of the closed glove; hitting below the belt, an imaginary line across the top of the hips, is a foul, and so is a punch to the kidneys (a change made in my time), on the back of the neck or head, or hitting a man when he's down. I don't think there are many people who don't know that a knock-out is a count of ten seconds, but nowadays you cannot be saved by the bell—the count is continued if it comes at the end of a round. The referee can also stop a bout if a boxer is injured, outclassed, or unfit to continue.

Professional boxing is much the same except for the number of rounds and the method of scoring. Novices box six rounds, then they are upgraded to eight and ten rounds. Elimination matches for a championship are twelve rounds, and title fights not less than fifteen rounds. In amateur boxing the referee is in the ring but he doesn't score. In pro boxing he makes a points verdict himself, as in Britain, or together with two judges outside the ring, as in America and Europe. In Britain the winner of any round gets five points. If he just loses he gets four and three quarters, if it's by a fair amount he gets four and a half. In Europe and America the maximum points are, respectively, five and ten for each round, with no fractions. There are one or two other important differences from country to country. As in amateur boxing, countries other than Britain allow a standing count by the referee, which means he goes on counting if the boxer is still dazed. Some American States still have a 'No foul' rule so that a boxer cannot be disqualified for breaking the rules. One of the strange parts of my career was that I never fought in America. The cards somehow never fell right, but one thing is for sure, they'd never have caught me in a no-foul ring. The bashed-in foul cup I got from Piero Tomasoni in my European title fight in 1969 is the only souvenir I want of that.

On the other hand I agree with the American system of ten points and, with some reservations, judges outside the ring. The splitting of numbers into fractions just seems stupid. Give it out of ten and if a man just loses a round you make it 10–9. Some even argue for 20–19, 20–18 and so on, but when all the playing with figures is done there is the very important principle of whether more than one opinion decides, and, just as important, whether the people doing the deciding have the experience and knowledge to assess the effect and quality of the boxer's work. Was it a clean punch? Where did it land? What was the strength of the blow? One good opinion would be better than three bad. But the referee has to control a fight, pulling the boxers out of clinches, stepping between them to stop the hitting on the break, warning them from time to time, and so on. Dodging around he sees more of some things than the judge sitting in one place, so while he should have his say in the verdict, I think he needs help. Nowadays, with television, there are millions of judges at home. Television gives you a slightly distorted picture in that you usually only see it from one side of the ring. It's a flat picture, no depth to it and, although a punch is sometimes missing, on television it looks as though it is landing. A fighter jerks his head back and the millions think it has hit him. In fact it hasn't. But everyone watching is a critic and has his view. That's why the sport is so popular, and you can't argue with that. But it's all the more reason why the people on the spot should have the best possible system to get the fairest verdict.

There are many ways in which amateur boxing differs from pro. As a pro you have to train for stamina and for a longer fight. You won't start off your fight as quickly as the amateur. You have to have a little bit more, let's face it. To my mind you've got to have a punch. You've got to know you can go into a ring and stop a man. Mentally it's nice to know that when you have a ten-round fight you don't have to go to the full ten rounds. When you are a puncher you perhaps think, 'I can end this in five or six rounds.' If you had to go ten to fifteen rounds, like it or not, you'd soon be saying to yourself, 'Oh, that again.' The knowledge that you have a punch gives you a terrific mental boost.

The two publics you have for amateur and professional boxing are totally different. The man who watches the amateurs is there mainly because he likes the sport, or is a friend or relative of one of the boxers. They're not nearly so knowledgeable as a professional crowd. It's a different type of boxing that is interesting them. Lots of short bouts and different opponents, which they enjoy. The professional fight crowd are a lot harder, and they like a little bet. They'll say, 'I'll have the red corner,' or 'You have the blue.' Even the ordinary chap will do that with his friend. The pro crowds are much more fickle, too, although how much this depends on the bets is hard to say. They shout and carry on more. Amateur crowds often have an MC telling them to keep quiet. Until fairly recently the referee sat outside the ring and they demanded quiet so that his shouts to the boxers could be heard. Also there was the tradition of the old National Sporting Club where you couldn't cheer your man during the round, only during the interval. The idea of this was taken to other places, where it just didn't go down, because boxing is a hard, exciting game, and people go there to enjoy themselves and get emotional. They can't sit there like a load of dummies. I think that's stupid. I don't believe in it. The crowd cheering on their man gives it all atmosphere. If you went into the ring and everything was dead silent you'd think you were in a morgue. It may be all right for the National Sporting Club, or one of the dinner-party clubs when you can hardly hear a murmur and over the loudspeaker you hear, 'Silence, please, during the rounds,' but to my mind it's not natural.

At Eltham we had a good and easy atmosphere, and I was just turned seventeen when I had a fight there which convinced me and a few others that I had a future in the game. It was against a former police champion, PC Trevillion. He was past his best, about thirty-two years old, so there was fifteen years between us, and when they made the match some thought he would have too much experience for me. But I went in there and I won, and I well won. It was a club show and this was a special contest of four three-minute rounds. I'd never done four rounds before and this guy was the National police champion in 1951. I could tell at once I was up against an experienced boxer. And he was a full-grown man while I was only a kid. I was a bit apprehensive, but Georgie Page said to me, 'They're all the same,' and while that's not exactly true the idea got over. I went in and won with my left hand. It was close, but there was no doubt that I had won. It was a big step in my career. To step out of junior into senior amateur boxing is one thing, but to step from there to beat a former police champion is another. People started to say, 'Henry's got something,' and I had a good little write-up in the local paper.

When I was still seventeen I won my first big competition, the Novices Open at Dartford. It also brought me one of the finest cups in my possession. They had got up this competition I think in the hope that Trevor Watkins, an Australian, and one of their star boxers, would win it. I'd beaten him once before, and three days before entries closed I entered my name. Watkins was a strong boy, and he and I reached the final. I beat him on points again and nicked the cup off him, much to their disappointment, I can't help feeling. Altogether I had four fights with Watkins, and each of them was good and hard. One day George and me went to a show, and they were saying to Watkins, 'We haven't got an opponent for you, do you want to fight Henry Cooper?' That was a bit much for Trevor. 'No thanks,' he said, 'he's beaten me four times already.' They then tried a different tack : 'His brother's here. What about him?' Watkins said, 'OK, that seems all right.' So George goes in and beats him as well! He could never get over us Coopers. He was a nice bloke, and when he went back to Australia our club presented him with an inscribed watch because in the four local shows in which he'd fought me he'd put up a hell of a good fight and the crowd loved him for it.

There was plenty doing in British heavyweight boxing in the 1950s and 1960s with Joe Erskine, Brian London, Dick Richardson, Peter Bates, Billy Walker, Jack Bodell, Johnny Prescott, Joe Bygraves, George and myself about. Joe Erskine and I developed a special rivalry, partly because we fought each other three times as amateurs.

I first met Joe in the light-heavyweight semi-finals of the ABA championships in April 1952. Already he was a good boxer technically, a good left jabber, a good mover, and a hard boy to box. He always seemed to be able to reach you. Whenever you thought you were out of distance, sure he couldn't sling a left hand, he did, the crafty so-and-so. When he was in distance you would think, he can't see my left or right coming, but he could. He was always unorthodox in that way. And he had a dead poker face. You could hit him and hurt him, and he would never show it. You'd wonder 'Have I hurt him?' and while you were thinking that, he would have recovered. He never showed any emotion in the ring.

Welsh boys like Joe were especially keen and good and there were a lot of them in those days. Every Welsh working man's club had a boxing section, the pits were encouraging it all the time, and all through the years they'd had good trainers, people like Frank Moody and Cyril and Alf Galley. South Wales was a great nursery of fighters, not great punchers as a rule, but clever boxers. Each area develops a tradition : South Wales, Belfast, East and South-east London, Birmingham, Wolverhampton, Derby, Nottingham,

Liverpool and Manchester, parts of Scotland, but not, so far as professional heavyweights go, Glasgow. That's one big industrial place that somehow misses out, although they've plenty of good boxers, mostly at the lighter weights.

Anyway, in the ABA semi-finals I got my left working well enough to beat Joe on points. He was a little bit unlucky because if we had been drawn in different halves I think he would have got through to the final. Joe Maclean, the Scot I met in the final, was strong and rugged but without much finesse. I don't think he would have beaten Joe, and I just jabbed away at him to win the title. I fought Joe Erskine twice more as an amateur, winning on points in October 1952 in the Army trials final, and then lost to him on points at the military boxing stadium at Aldershot. I was dead hot favourite to win in our team, and I was the only one who didn't. I remember that all right.

Basil Kew I also met three times as an amateur. I beat him twice and he beat me once. You could hit him with everything, even the stool in the corner, and you still couldn't make much impression on him. I remember I fought him once at an open air show in Ladywell recreation ground. It was a beautiful summer's day but it was a right bloodbath. He had a nose bleed from early on, then I had one, and we were both smothered in blood. A little blood can go a long way, like when you spill the tea, but it was more than a splatter or two that day. It was a special four-round fight, and special just about covered it. We were always great friends and afterwards it made not the slightest difference to us. Basil turned professional but finished early. He turned pro a little too late. He had the wrong style for the pro game and he wasn't able to change. As a pro you had plenty of boys who were tough and strong. Whereas Basil could wear an amateur down and win a few fights, as a pro he could only expect to make up the bill and please the crowd. Like Billy Walker and Mark Rowe he was prepared to take two punches and land one. There's a balance of payments for that sort of style. Fighters like that have only so many fights in them. They've got to realise that they are only in the game for a limited period of time. If they go on and on they'll end up on their heels. The human frame is not made to stand that sort of punishment.

The best fighter I fought as an amateur was one of the

least known in Britain, Tony Madigan. He was an Australian, and he came over here especially to win an ABA title. When I met him in the 1953 ABA light-heavyweight final, he'd stopped every boy in every round he'd had. He was dead hot favourite to win although I was the champion from 1952. He was a hell of a puncher, and tough, and I thought it the best fight I had won—it was on points. He went back to Australia and stayed amateur throughout his career, winning an Empire Games Gold Medal, the Golden Gloves in America, and an Olympic Games Silver Medal. It was that win over Madigan which convinced me that when I got out of the Army I would turn professional.

George meantime had been fighting heavyweight all the time. The light-heavyweight limit was 12 stone 10, and in the early days I was well short of that, around 12 stone 4. to 6. But towards the end of my amateur career while I was in the Army I started putting on weight and I had a big job keeping under the limit. I wanted to do that so as to keep out of George's division. Naturally we would have loved him to win the ABA heavyweight title. He was a heavier puncher than me—he stopped more boys with his right hand than I ever did. I had eighty-four senior amateur bouts and I won seventy-three and lost eleven. George had sixty-four and he won forty-two and lost twenty-two. In those forty-two wins he had a better average of KOs than I did. A lot of his fights never got beyond the first round. Towards the end of my Army career I was stopping them more. Of the last twenty fights I suppose ten were wins inside the distance, either by a knock-out or with the referee stopping the contest. My weight, timing, strength and know-how were improving all the time. I was lucky. I stayed fit, but George suffered badly from cut eyes. He has sharper, more prominent brow and cheek bones than me. He only needed a tap on his eyebrow and it would be cut. Eventually he went to Queen Victoria Hospital at East Grinstead where they specialise in plastic surgery, and he had the edge of the eyebrow taken right off.

He was also unluckier than me in that at sixteen he had scarlet fever which developed into rheumatic fever. He was in a fever hospital flat on his back for nearly three months. He couldn't wash himself, they had to feed him intravenously, and it was only because he was an athlete with a

46

strong heart that he was able to come out of it so well. But he lost a year's boxing, and it was remarkable that he was able to come out of the Army and turn professional. Then in one of his last amateur bouts he hit a guy on the head so hard that he broke his thumb. It was broken in two places, but that wasn't the end of it. When they brought him back for a check after setting it they found there was a bit of bone floating where it hadn't set properly. They had to put him out, break it and reset it. They did that three times, and eventually they said it still wasn't right, but it was the best they could do. George never punched so hard again.

CHAPTER FIVE

The Olympic Games at Helsinki in July 1952 was my first big international event. They took us to RAF Benson in Oxfordshire for a fortnight's special training. Alf Galley was in charge of training and Fred Verlander his assistant. I was pretty lucky. We couldn't really afford for me to be off work for six weeks, but Mum was working at the time, and she said : 'If you want to do it, you do it.' I was away six weeks all told and Mum financed me entirely from her charring. I suppose that made me a true-blue amateur all right! In those days athletes were not given any spending money or allowed broken time at Olympic Games, and it came very hard if you were from a working-class home. In Helsinki we lived in flats which they had just built and afterwards were going to be rented out by the city council. On one floor all of us were boxers. Above us were the wrestlers and below us the fencers. It was a great experience. I enjoyed the community living, but those Games were more political than most. The Russians had a separate village of their own and whenever they came to the boxing hall they did so in a private coach. They were ushered into their own special dressing-room and you never had a chance to talk to them even through an interpreter. Directly their bouts were finished they went straight back, no chatting in the shower as you did with the others. I had a bye in the first round, much to my delight, and then I was up against a Russian, Anatoli Perov. I knew nothing about him, but we had a good bout which I thought I just won. But there were two judges from Communist countries and one from France. The Frenchman gave the fight to me, but the other two gave it to the Russian, so I was out on a split decision.

This was the greatest Olympic boxing show ever. The Americans had a wonderful team. At flyweight they had Nate Brooks, who won the title and made the pro grade, though he had a tragically early end. Then there was Spider Webb, Floyd Patterson, boxing then at middleweight and winning the Gold, and Novel Lee, who won my light-heavy division. The heavyweight champion was Ed Sanders, a great big fellow who would have made the pro grade, but he died of a brain haemorrhage. Altogether the Americans won five of the ten Gold Medals in that Olympics.

As well as the Americans there was Laszlo Papp, of Hungary, who won the light-middleweight Gold, Willee Toweel, of South Africa, and Ingemar Johansson. Johansson, if you can believe it now, was slung out of the ring for not trying! Patterson at that time was very fast, very flashy, the same style as he had later only faster. He looked so good in winning the Gold Medal you simply thought: 'Blimey, here's a good fighter.' I couldn't understand, though, why the British boxers did so badly compared with the East European countries, the Poles, Russians, Hungarians and East Germans especially. In 1908 Britain won all five Olympic classes, and until the 1930s played a big part in every Games. Here we had no Golds although our boxers had much better techniques than the East Europeans. True they were fit and strong, but we should have done better.

I never did any good in the Olympic Games or in the European Championships. In May 1953 I'd won my second ABA title by beating Madigan and was as confident as could be. But in the European Championships in Warsaw I fought another Russian, Juri Jegorow, and I copped one in my first fight in the very first round. Halfway through the round and, bang! he hit me, and though I wasn't knocked out I was groggy, and the referee stopped the fight. Looking back to both events I suppose the atmosphere was different, it was a big occasion, and I got too tense. Still, it should have been the same for the other guy. There isn't much excuse. I hadn't learned to relax, to leave the worrying to others. That came much later.

Two days after arriving back from the Olympic Games full of travellers' tales I was Private Henry Cooper, RAOC. George and me joined the Royal Army Ordnance Corps at Blackdown, just outside Aldershot. We'd planned to join the Scots Guards, being tall fellows, but one evening at a boxing tournament in London a Captain Eastlake introduced himself. He asked what we were going to do in the Army during our National Service and when we said the Scots Guards he said: 'But you won't get any boxing with them. Why don't you come and join us?' We had never heard of 4 Battalion, RAOC, but Captain Eastlake used to earmark all the London boxers for what the Army had good reason to call the Boxers' Battalion. We went to Blackdown for six weeks' square bashing, then we went down the road half a mile to Deep Cut, where 4 Battalion had its headquarters, to take a driving course. That was very handy and I never had need of a driving school afterwards.

After six weeks on Austin three-tonners we joined the battalion proper. I did very little soldiering, I must confess. If I did two guard duties all the time I was in the Army that might be an exaggeration. It took a little while before it sank in what life was all about there. One day at Blackdown I was in the classroom learning all about motors when the instructor suddenly called out, 'Cooper, Sergeant-Major Cavanagh wants to speak to you.' I jumped up thinking to myself, 'What have I done? Didn't I look at orders last night?' As I stood to attention there was the sergeant-major with the peak of his cap right over his forehead and his stick under his arm, looking very fierce. 'Oh Lord,' I thought, 'what now?' He says, 'Don't you remember me? Cavanagh? You boxed me a couple of months ago.' I said: 'Cor blimey, yes.' Of all people I'd had to knock out the Company Sergeant-Major when he fought for Birkenhead against Eltham in an amateur boxing match.

He was the nicest guy going. He was in charge of all the boxers of 4 Battalion. On parade in the morning, it was 'Boxers . . . Fall out!' And we were straight up to the gym, thank you very much. We had the time of our life for the first year. When CSM Cavanagh had to leave things got a bit stricter, but we still only basically boxed or trained for boxing. The War Office must have known, but it was a bit of prestige and publicity for recruitment, I suppose. In the end, though, it got to such a pitch that 4 Battalion won the Army team championship six years on the trot, and other units got a bit narked being beaten by what really was an international team. In National Service days the Army was much bigger than it is now, but we'd go into inter-unit matches and still win 11–0 or 10–1. If we only won 9–2 there'd be murders. 'What's happening to us? Why have we slipped?' It got such that we eventually had to break up, some going to Chilwell and some to Wales.

We had Joe Erskine, me, George, Dennis and Ronnie Hinson, Eddie Woollard, Nicky Gargagno, all of us turning pro afterwards. For a while Joe and me were in the same billet, though since we were the same weight they eventually shifted him to another unit. I got to know him well. We would sit and play cards—a great card sharp, Joe. There was another fighter, Darkie Best, and these two would play with each other so that you weren't playing one, you were playing two. They didn't mess about! They'd throw in two bob and take out change for half a crown if you didn't look lively. I'd say: 'Come on, Joe, what's your game? Who are we playing? You or both of you?' Right villains they were over a card game!

We were home every weekend, and boxing in London twice a week at London club shows. The neighbours got to know our routine pretty well in Farmstead Road. A quick whip round from Mum and Dad on the Sunday night brought us about six bob if we were lucky, then out of the house at 4 am to be back at the billet for first parade. It wasn't too bad a life but we wanted to get out of the Army. George and me were never born soldiers and in any case we were laying plans for turning professional. There were two main writers on amateur boxing at the time, Wally Bartleman, then on the old *Star*—he lives right opposite me in Wembley—and J. T. Hulls, of the *Evening News*. We called them the Two Musketeers. They were always together at the Army and London amateur boxing shows. Every Sunday before we joined up old J.T. used to come up from Hayes in Kent to see us, walking all the way from the station. Often he'd miss us because we were at training, but he'd sit down and Mum would make him a cup of coffee. He was a good old stick, and he would always say: 'If the boys are going to turn professional there's only one man to

manage them—Jim Wicks. He's the best of them. I'll make
the introduction for you.' So one evening before we went
into the Army we took a 160 bus and then got another bus
to Bexleyheath as we usually did for training, but this time
we called in to see Mr Wicks, who lived in Footscray Road,
Eltham. Georgie Page, our trainer, was with us, but we
didn't know quite what to expect. I suppose we had visions
of a boxing manager looking something like Noel Coward,
with a cigarette in a holder and a silk dressing-gown. But
the Wickses seemed such a homely pair—his wife was only
a little woman, about as tall as Albina. It was the sort of
home like our own home in Farmstead Road. I got to know
Mrs Wicks much better later, and she would always say to
me : 'You look after your money, son. It's hard earned.'
And Jim has always been just great. It was the wisest move
we ever made. We were young boys, we didn't know anything, but we weren't full of conceit. Rather the opposite.
We didn't think : 'We're going to earn thousands of pounds
as professional boxers.' All we wanted to do was make the
grade, perhaps earn £40 for our first fight and help Mum a
bit more than we had been doing. We were putting our
future in a stranger's hands, but straightaway we sensed
that the welfare of Jim's boxers came first. Although boxing
is a hard business he was interested in you.

If he'd been interested in the money he would have said
there and then, 'All right, I've contracts here. You sign
these.' But he didn't. He put us right. He said : 'If you go
into the Army as professionals you won't get any conces-
sions. If you box for them as an amateur you'll go here,
there and everywhere. As a pro you won't be allowed to box
for them.' This was going right against his own interests. As
he says, it could have been the biggest mistake of his life. In
the Army, particularly towards the end, there were managers
coming up right, left and centre offering us the Crown
Jewels to sign with them. We told them all, 'No, we're going
with Jim Wicks.' That was it. We hadn't signed anything
with him. But Jim had advised us well from the very first
and when we came out of the Army we went straight away
to see him. Jim had first seen me against Madigan in the
1953 ABA final. He reckoned I had a good left hand and
moved correctly against a strong two-handed fighter. But he
didn't know me and never in his life did he reckon to run

51

after a fighter. When Jimmy Hulls rang him up to say he wanted us to see him it gave him quite a surprise. He had almost forgotten us.

In my amateur career I was lucky that Eltham was such a well-run club. As with all committees or clubs, there are one or two people who make the whole thing go. Eltham had Tom Smith, the competitions secretary, and Georgie Page—even when we turned pro he trained us for a time. Eltham was a new baths—with decent changing accommodation and a nice refreshment place. They were enjoyable years with a good amateur club atmosphere. They would run coach outings when we were fighting in North London or anywhere down by the coast, and you'd all have a sing-song on the way there and back. As kids we loved that. It was boxing for fun. In professional boxing you still try to conduct yourself in a sporting way, but basically it's a business. You're in it for the hard cash. It's not everywhere as mercenary as some might think. I enjoyed professional boxing, too, and I would do it all again. I certainly would never discourage young Henry and John from taking up amateur boxing. Professional is a different thing—fundamentally you've got to be good enough. Amateur boxing has all the critics in the world but I still say it is character building, and it's a shame that fewer schools are encouraging it. It's good to get the kids off the street corners and going into the gym. It's good to have a training routine which provides a discipline quite aside from the obvious physical improvements. But where boxing is chiefly character building is in the ring, where no kid can afford to lose his temper. If he does, nine times out of ten he'll be punished more. You go berserk and, bonk!—your opponent is just picking you off. When new kids came into the club you could sometimes tell they only wanted the glory, to be able to boast to their mates, 'I'm a boxer, I belong to Eltham Boxing Club.' But you could sort a bully from the boxer. You'd put him in with a pretty useful kid. You wouldn't take advantage, but you'd let the useful boy get in one or two digs. All novices are out of breath pretty quickly, and if you get a tap in the tummy in that condition then you think you're spine is collapsing. If the kid turned up again the next week you'd know he was keen. I guarantee eight out of ten wouldn't come back.

George and me went through all that mill. In the early days I was about eight or nine stone, and I was in against this kid of seven and a half stone. He was no thicker than my little finger, and I thought : 'He'll do. Lovely.' I went in like a bull in a china shop, but this kid was a schoolboy champion, and I had more left hands in my face than I ever thought possible. While he belted me I never landed a glove on him. But George and me were keen and we went back the next week.

Some element of physical danger I think is necessary in most lives. The human being just wasn't built as a vegetable. There is this tendency now to an over-protective society. If there is danger in anything some people want to ban it—you mustn't box, you mustn't climb mountains, you mustn't race fast cars. Nothing would have been achieved in the world if there wasn't a determination to beat an element of danger or challenge. You must keep the danger down to something that's reasonable. Risk-taking ought to be a calculated thing. No boxer will get seriously injured if he goes into the ring properly matched, fit and trained up. Fighters know it. Tragedies happen when they are not 100 per cent fit or have shirked their training. Sometimes they may be hiding an injury, perhaps from themselves. A brain haemorrhage is an exception. But that's a basic weakness which is put at risk unknown to the boxer. He could just as easily suffer the haemorrhage by banging his head on the cupboard under the stairs or against a lamp post. I would say on a good many occasions when a boxer is simply knocked out then he knows he should have done more training. There are other things in pro boxing that can go wrong, and you need to be constantly on guard against them. A boxer can be badly managed. He can take the wrong sort of opposition. There are fighters Jim Wicks would never have taken for me. The game is in constant need of criticism and self-criticism. Given the control, boxing is a good game.

The British Boxing Board of Control must always be kept up to the mark by the press and the public, though I do firmly believe that boxing in Britain is the best run in the world. Boxers are examined frequently here—they can't be examined enough. If you're stopped with a cut eye, and it happened to me a few times, you've got to present the Board of Control with a doctor's certificate saying you are fit to box again. If you are knocked out you are automatically suspended for twenty-one days, and then you have to produce another doctor's certificate. If you are knocked out three times the boxer and manager have to appear before the Board of Control. Each year when his licence is reviewed, a boxer has a detailed medical report to fill in from his doctor. Then before every fight a boxer is examined by the Board doctor at the weigh-in. I am not saying this is foolproof. But he grips your hand, and if there is anything broken he'll know. You are checked for a hernia or a rupture, they sound your chest, they look at your eyes, they tell you to put your feet together, close your eyes and bend down. If you did that and fell over obviously there would be something pretty seriously wrong. You certainly wouldn't get by if you had flu. Most of the precautions are adequate here, but I cannot say the same for America. Every State there has a separate commission. If I am banned in New York I can cross a State line or two and get a fight. It's even been known with boxers suffering from a detached retina. That's why some of them end up blind. In Europe you have to have an up-to-date medical certificate signed by your national boxing board of control or they won't let you box. That reduces the area of risk. The procedures before fights in Italy and Germany are much the same as ours.

Although I never met Baroness Summerskill until after I finished boxing, I knew her as a fervent opponent of it and read her views. It always seemed to me that she based her facts on boxing of years ago. If she was campaigning fifty or seventy years back I might have agreed with her. Jimmy Wilde had six hundred fights. If you were absorbing a dozen to twenty blows each fight your lumps and bumps and cauliflower ears would certainly be showing after six hundred. The body isn't built to withstand that sort of punishment. Nowadays there aren't that number of fighters so you can't have all those fights. And there are much better medical safeguards. But Edith Summerskill still comes out with statements that 'after eighty fights a fighter's speech starts to slur,' or 'after one hundred fights so and so, and so and so.' Her figures are out of proportion. In nearly seventeen years of professional boxing I had fifty-five fights, and I went on longer than most.

What else had I learned as an amateur, and what had I

still to learn? I had became accustomed to the big occasion, and knew I enjoyed it. George Page had seen the potential in my left hand, and polished me up. I had a good left jab and a fairish left hook. He'd set us both on the road. But now it was going to be a different kind of game. Where amateur was sprint, professional was distance. We had to build a lot more stamina which meant much more roadwork and heavy training. The hardest thing for a professional boxer is to learn how to pace himself. I think I learned it pretty quickly, but many boxers never learn. They flare up over four or five rounds, and towards the end of a fifteen-round fight they are puffing and panting. You have to know how to sum up your opponent, his strength and his weaknesses. As an amateur you never study your opponent; at least I never did. Perhaps I should have done. If he was a well-known fighter you simply knew him, you had no particular strategy. You just fought your fight. In professional fighting you will know, or your manager or your trainer will tell you, this fellow is open to a right hand, or a left hook, and so you exploit a man's weakness.

CHAPTER SIX

Jim Wicks had a tremendous knack for publicity. Many times in my career when things were quiet and we were in the doldrums Jim would think up something he knew the newspapermen would like. The fact that me and George were twins was a novelty Jim realised at once he could play up. He rang Peter Dimmock, who at that time was introducing *Sportsview* on BBC television, and told him he was signing us professional. They arranged that we would box a round, then come out of the ring and sit down and sign the contract with millions of people watching. That was the first time it was done in this country. In those days all sorts of sporting celebrities would appear on the same programme, and that night there were Peter May, Gordon Richards, Freddie Winter, Tony Lock and Jim Laker. Only one thing went wrong. The temporary ring they had rigged up fell down while we were boxing. Jim couldn't fool us it was part of the act, either!

I had my last amateur fight in April 1954, and then it was a case of settling to my new routine before my first pro fight in September. Some of my life remained the same. We were still working as plasterers, but I could get time off easily enough. George and me still shared the same bedroom in Farmstead Road—in different beds by now, of course—with Bern married and left home. He had met Cory at a dance. She is a Welsh girl, the daughter of a miner who died of silicosis, and her mother lives in Barry. They were courting for a couple of years before they married and went to live in Catford.

Our gym was Jim Wicks's place at the Thomas a' Beckett pub in the Old Kent Road. There we trained for the first year or so under both Georgie Page and Danny Holland, Jim's trainer. Jim had quite a stable at the time. There was Alex Buxton from Watford, the light-heavyweight champion, Jake Tuli the Empire bantamweight champion, and Joe Lucy the British lightweight champion. All three were being trained by Danny. Jim also had a light-heavyweight, Brian Anders, from Brighton, who helped us a great deal. He wasn't a great puncher but he was one of the cagiest boys around. In particular he taught us how to ride punches.

From April to September we were in the ring three or four times a week with him. We would train most days. We had a very good relationship with Reg Reynolds, who would give us a half-day or an hour or two off at the end of the day so that we could get to the Thomas a' Beckett for evening training. Reg was a plastering contractor with about ten men working for him and he was very decent about things —he would often arrange his work schedules to help us. We had an old banger by then, the Ford Prefect, but it was paid for out of plastering rather than boxing. We got nothing at all for signing. Jim had never bought a boxer in his life, and I'm glad he never did. He got us our boxing gear, bought us our first satin pants, and so on, but he never said here's a thousand for turning pro. Jim reckoned that guys who did that were only concerned with getting their money back first. They would not be considering their boy enough. If a promoter said to that sort of manager, 'I want your boy to fight so-and-so for five hundred quid,' the manager would be working out his whack and agreeing to the fight even though he might know his boy wasn't ready for it.

Because Jim never gave us money he picked and chose our opponents without any pressures from the promoters. Otherwise we signed the standard Board of Control contract. It states that the manager takes twenty-five per cent of the boxer's money after all expenses have been deducted. We signed the first one for three years and didn't sign another again. Between Jim and us there was an affection quite different to the normal boxer–manager relationship. We were more like father and sons. Our contract ran out and we never knew. No one could have nicked us off Jim. It never arose. He is the greatest so far as we are concerned. If Jim had packed up I would have finished with boxing. It was as simple as that.

To build our stamina we really went to work on the road. As amateurs we ran two miles about twice a week. Now we had to be on the road every day, either in the morning or evening, depending how it suited our other work. And we ran not two miles but four or five, in about forty to forty-five minutes, every day of the week except Sundays. We were grateful we'd been so active when we were kids. We were always chasing about in Beckenham Park and Beckenham Wood, one gang after the other, I suppose doing about ten miles in the normal playing day, up hill, down dale. You never thought about it as training, but it made things that much easier when we got down to pro boxing under Jim.

We didn't begin with any conscious campaign. We took our fights one at a time, leaving Jim to decide whom we fought. He knew so much about it, he would simply say to us that this boy or that should suit us, and we accepted it. There was no consultation. Jim it was who chose Harry Painter for my first fight. He had been a pretty useful boxer but he was a little past his best. for an up-and-coming boy like myself this was the right time to take him. The fight was in the old Harringay Arena in north London—three of our first four fights were there. It was a marvellous arena, octagon shaped so that everyone could see, and always with a good atmosphere. It was totally different from the amateur game. Everything was much bigger, and the smell was so different with so many of the guys smoking cigars. We were only a six-rounder, going on before the main bill. Naturally I was a bit nervous, wanting to show everyone I was some good, but Jim was saying in the dressing-room, 'Now take it easy. Relax. Don't try to over-impress.' He didn't say now go in there and hit this guy with this and that. He didn't load up our brains. 'It'll all come to you as you go along,' he said.

Harry Painter was tall and sandy-haired, a lot heavier than me at 14 stone 13. He'd won one of Jack Solomons's heavyweight novices' competitions, but that was some way back. He was a bit cumbersome, without a lot of finesse in spite of his experience, and I soon found I could jab him fairly easily as he came in at me. About halfway through the first round I caught him with a good left hand to the chin and he went down. He got up, but I knocked him down again and it was all over. George went on afterwards and beat Dick Richardson on points, which set us both off on the right foot, but though we were all well pleased we just went quietly home—no riotous celebrations. Between us we had £70 in our pockets from the purse and £35 expenses, and we went straight off and bought Mum and Dad their first television set. We were teetotallers then, in fact neither of us had even had a glass of beer. Nor were we smokers. As kids we did the usual things. On Bellingham, the only cigarettes you seemed to be able to get during the war were Nosegay Specials. They were as black as your shoes and as strong as hell. One day on the way to the pictures we bought ten and, kids being kids, we couldn't keep anything in our pockets for long. So we had to smoke them all, and we all stumbled out before the main film was finished, sick as dogs. There were three of us, we smoked two or three each, and we thought we'd killed ourselves. That put me off for life. I never touched another cigarette again.

For about a year or so Georgie Page and Danny Holland got on well with each other in training us. But eventually the things that Georgie disliked about professional boxing began to get on top. He was a great trainer of amateurs, and he was a true-blue amateur at heart himself. I suppose to some he was a rough sort of diamond, but he'd devoted loads of time to youth clubs. He wanted a gym of his own just to train me, but you couldn't do that. There were always other guys who had every right to be there, besides the hangers-on. There's a slickness about the professional game which George disliked, and after a while the atmosphere got too much for him and he turned it in. Danny had been a trainer for many years. He was at the old Torbay Gymnasium before Jim brought him in to train his boxers. Both he and Georgie were about fifty at the time. Danny we knew nothing about until we met him through Jim, but we got on well straight away, and for about fourteen years after that, with Danny doing some marvellous work as the cut man in my corner. Towards the end there was a bit of unpleasantness and we parted. But these things happen; they happen in all businesses.

For the first eighteen months we never addressed Jim Wicks in any other way than Mr Wicks this and Mr Wicks that. We had been brought up to respect our elders, but eventually he turned round one day in the gym and said, 'That's enough of the Mr Wicks. Call me Jim.' Some of the newspapermen called him the Bishop, because of his shiny bald head, pink cheeks, and his way of talking, and quite a few of his friends Seamus, because of his Irish blood. Originally he was a bookmaker; in fact he taught Jack Solomons a great deal about that game. They opened a business up in Panton Street together, but later they split up and Jim concentrated on boxing. Jack Solomons, of course, went in for boxing promotion, and was the No 1 until Harry Levene built up. How Jim handled both of them was an important part of our boxing life later on.

The other important person in our lives at the time was of course Reg Reynolds. He was the man who was teaching us the plastering craft in case, for any reason, our boxing failed. George, today, with his own business at Farningham in Kent, has special reasons for being grateful to him, because later on he married Reg's daughter, Barbara. At first we were simply labouring for Reg, but then he taught us how to mix plaster as he wanted it. He would lay some stuff on and then he would let us trowel it up a bit. And he would show us when to flick more water on, how to level, plumb and scree. In those days we were using sand, cement and lime, which was really heavy. But it was certainly an asset to our boxing because it developed our trunks, arms and shoulders where we most needed it. My left hand was my trowel hand, and it was all pushing. When you'd had a whole day plastering you would come home really beat.

But, as I've explained, we were no sooner home than we were washed, changed, had eaten a quick tea and were off again to our boxing training. The whole thing gave us our stamina. In the end, though, the boxing became too demanding and after eighteen months of my professional career I had to give up plastering.

Altogether I had a pretty encouraging start. I won the first five fights by knock-outs or the ref stopping the fight, three of them in the first round. In fact I won the first nine, but in the tenth I had my first cut eye and the thirteenth also proved unlucky—I was beaten over ten rounds by Joe Erskine. That was on November 15, 1955. But things generally went very nicely. My second fight was against Dinny Powell, brother of Nosher, the great comedian of the game in those days. They would always put Nosher on last because they knew the crowd would stay to the very end to see him perform. Dinny had been around. He was shorter and stockier than me, but he knew the game and it was the first time I came across anyone waggling his old head so as to try and bump your eye and perhaps get a cut going—another of the reasons why I say pro boxing is a harder game. Anyway, I stopped him in the fourth round and then went on to KO Ted Keith in the first, Denny Ball in the third, and Colin Strauch in the first.

But at Harringay on February 8, 1955, I had another lesson coming up. Cliff Purnell was the first southpaw I had fought professionally—I hadn't boxed too many as an amateur. This guy was really awkward, though in the end I won on points. Southpaws have a big advantage. The orthodox boxer meets one about once a pancake day. But southpaws are fighting orthodox boxers all the time. Their right arm and right foot come up against your left, and you never look good. You always expect them to go one way and they go the other. Their left arm and foot so often seem to get behind you somehow, and you go back and you're falling over them. An orthodox boxer only ever seems to look OK against one when he catches him with a really good punch. You do best against them by hitting with the right hand. I was a left-hand merchant, in those days especially, when I was mostly straight punching and before I had developed the left hook. I might have seen an opportunity, but suddenly it was gone with me saying to myself, 'Why wasn't I there?'—though you could say that for various reasons of most fights.

Looking back in those early days, my outstanding weakness, or ignorance, concerned my weight. In the first four fights I was about 13 stone 7 pounds, but in the last two I was getting slightly heavier, 13 stone 9, and against Purnell 13–9½. Later on I found that that was too heavy for me. The great secret of boxing is to find your best fighting weight. A lot of people think that if you are a heavyweight you can come in at any weight. Well, you can, but you are deceiving yourself if you think you haven't a best fighting weight, and if you discover that early it's a big advantage. I found that 13 stone 7½ was best for me. A couple of pounds in 190 may not seem much, just a packet of sugar on the table, maybe. But if I was 13 stone 9, 10 or 11, I was slow and sluggish, and my reactions were too slow. If I came in at 13–7½ I could move sharply and I had the weight there for punching.

My ninth fight, and best victory so far, was against Joe Bygraves. I hadn't met him before, but he had been in the same team as me on a famous, or some would say infamous, boxing occasion. I was light-heavyweight and he was heavyweight in an England amateur team fighting against Wales. We travelled down with a referee called Mr English. He refereed only two fights in the match—involving me and Joe Bygraves—and disqualified us both. That was the time when as the referee came into the dressing-room Joe chinned him—knocked him spark out—and straightaway turned pro. He didn't have much alternative, because they banned him from amateur boxing for life. Joe was my first eight-round fight, and it was in a charity show at Manor Place Baths for Walworth old age pensioners—Jack Solomons used to run it every year. I boxed well in that—I had him down in the last round and nearly had him out. Joe was a big guy, near enough 15 stone, and a real muscle man. Jet black, too, he looked really fierce. I was told, 'Don't mix it. Jab and move. Pick your punches.' In fact I found that Joe tired pretty badly.

George was always on the same bill as me. He was getting some good results but his usual quota of bad luck. Cut eyes were bothering him more than they were me. He lost seven of his first fourteen professional fights because of them.

We knew from his amateur days that he was more vulnerable. I think people sometimes confuse the two of us on this. I had my troubles with cuts, but in my whole pro career I lost only four fights specifically because of a cut. And the first of those occasions was coming up. This was against the Italian, Uber Bacilieri, the first foreign boxer I'd fought, at the Harringay Arena, and the upsetting thing was that I was boxing so blooming well when it happened. Suddenly in the second there was a clash of heads, wallop! — and I came out with a cut eye. Jim Wicks stopped it fairly quickly, for though it wasn't a bad cut as eyes go, I was just coming up and Jim wasn't going to risk another knock.

Bacilieri was a good boxer, a good mover, though not a great puncher. He had won the Italian title but wasn't all that old. I found him fairly orthodox but, like most Continentals, he held his hands high — the peekaboo style as we called it. Jim warned me about this. We knew it meant I should jab to the body to try and bring his hands down. But Jim never told you a lot before the first round. He would just say, 'Be careful. Just feel him out.' Then after the second or third rounds he would tell you things. This time he didn't get the chance because it was all over in the second. The cut was in the brow. My cuts were always there or in the lid on the left, or leading side. We were a little bit worried, but Danny was a good cut man and he worked on it straight away and stopped the bleeding. I had no stitches.

Danny had developed the cut business to a fine art. He would get the adrenalin out and opened as soon as he saw a cut, and he had the cotton swab stick out and in the bottle with his thumb over the top. He made the swab stick beforehand in the dressing room, so he was all ready to jump straight up in the ring and, without wasting time unscrewing bottle lids, to get to work. He never used a sponge. It makes me wince to see some people, amateurs especially, wiping a cut with a wet sponge. That's the worst thing you can do, because you get water in the cut. Danny always had dry, clean towels, cotton swabs, and an adrenalin and vaseline mixture ready. He'd pinch the cut together, wiping the surplus blood away, lay the swabs gently onto the cut, then apply the adrenalin and vaseline compound to seal it. The adrenalin would stop the bleeding by congealing the blood. And that was it. If you swab with water first it just dilutes the adrenalin and it won't stop the bleeding. In America and on the Continent they use a brand of solution which I think is deadly. It'll stop the bleeding quicker because it's a cement and it hardens in the wound, but before a doctor can treat the cut he has to chisel all that stuff out. It's illegal over here. You can always tell when it's being used abroad because the blood turns jet black.

The big secret of the good cut man is speed. Some people get in the corner and they're fiddling about with the bottle, unscrewing the lid, dipping in. That's ten to fifteen seconds being wasted. You get a minute between rounds but, once the bell goes, from the time you get to the corner and your men are up that's eight seconds gone, even if you've tried to end the round near your own corner. So you've only about fifty seconds in which to work. If you're fiddling about for ten seconds then you're down to not much over half a minute. Danny would always get on with his work before anyone did anything else, like taking your gum shield out. We had a good way of working the corner. Jim would always let Danny up the stairs and inside the ropes first, Jim was next, then the water carrier, George, was third. We'd have ice packs in the corner to stop the swelling on a bruised eye coming up quickly, but we would never use it for the treatment of bruises afterwards. We would have hot towels. I'd dip a towel into water as hot as I could bear, wring it out, then lay it on the bruise steaming hot. I'd then massage the bruise away. I could look pretty terrible during and after a fight, but three or four days afterwards I guarantee you wouldn't see a bruise. I had very quick-healing skin only because I used to work it with hot towels. A lot of people believe in ice packs. I don't. Ice packs slow down the circulation and congeal the blood, whereas heat quickens the blood. After all a bruise is only congealed blood and heat gets it away into the system. Fighters who use ice packs a lot have all got lumps and bumps but I never had. You could use ice packs during the fight, but I wouldn't touch them afterwards.

As for nose injuries, there's very little you can do during a fight except put an adrenalin stick up your nostril, but it is blooming uncomfortable and it restricts your breathing. If the damage is high up you won't stop it in any case. I always believe in letting a nose-bleed bleed, which means breathing through your mouth. I didn't have much nose trouble. I never had a broken nose, nor did I have a prominent bridge to my nose to catch trouble. I don't seem to have much bone in my nose at all; it's all gristle. I was fortunate in that respect. I've two clear nostrils and could always breathe properly. When people break their nose it seems to bung up one side or the other and they have difficulty in breathing at times.

After blows to the solar plexus, most seconds pull the shorts away from the boxer's stomach as he sits in the corner — shorts have very tight elastic — and that eases the breathing. If you've copped one or two light blows to the body they will lightly massage your stomach. That's about all you can do. In my early years of pro boxing you were allowed to punch on the break, and that was my strong suit. Coming out of the clinch I used to love getting one in, but they banned that, goodness knows why, in later years. Kidney punching, round the back, that's bad, and it's illegal, but I could throw a nice little left hook to the liver. I've had guys literally scream out at that. They used to go down paralysed. I've won a good many fights that way. I remember once a Spanish boxer employed by Jim as a sparring partner. In the first round I noticed that every time we came away from a clinch he would drop his hands. I told Bobby Diamond, the Spaniard's agent, to get him to keep his hands up or I would catch him on the chin. So next round he comes out with his hands high up, exposing all his stomach. I gave him a hell of a left hook to the liver and he literally screamed and fell on the floor. Directly he was fit enough to get up he leapt out of the ring, ripped his gloves off without undoing the laces, tore off his headguard and rushed to the dressing-room. He didn't stop for a shower, and that was the last we ever saw of him. He didn't even stop for his money, though Bobby probably caught up with him later.

I've been hit to the liver and kidneys many a time. As I've explained, any clean shot, any great knock-out punch, doesn't seem to hurt. It's some of the in-between punches that give you pain. It happens, for example, when a guy who is a good puncher slings a long one, and you just come inside it, but you catch it on the eye or the back of the neck. That neck blow, especially, really shakes your head. It seems to make your head vibrate. It hurts much more than a

64

short, sharp, clean blow. In cartoon films or strips they sometimes show a character hitting his head and everything goes bong-bong-bong and you get about six impressions. That's exactly how it is when you get one at the back of the neck. It hurts when you bang the bridge of the nose, but a boxer isn't often caught there, he's bobbing around so much. All you've really got to worry about when you cop a punch on the nose is your eyes watering!

CHAPTER SEVEN

On September 13, 1955, I had my revenge on Bacilieri, with a knock-out in the seventh round, but two months later I was back on my heels again with my first real defeat, by Joe Erskine over ten rounds at Harringay. It was, as I have said, my thirteenth pro fight. Joe was always a hard guy to knock out of his stride once he was allowed to settle down. On this occasion he kidded me—instead of me going out from the first bell and being the governor I thought I'd take my time and get a second wind. But once Joe got going I couldn't shift him. I caught him with a few good punches but Joe had this poker face, he just rolled his head and shut his eyes, and you didn't know whether you'd hurt him or not. The greatest kidder out was old Joe. In my notes on that fight I've got 'injured left hand in the seventh round.' I did it hitting the top of Joe's hard head. He would put his head down and you could hit him everywhere except the place you wanted—on the chin. Joe was a lot harder guy to fight than most of the heavyweights going around at that time. I'd sooner have fought London and Richardson than Erskine. London and Richardson were big strong guys but they had only one way of fighting, coming in and trying to knock you straight up in the air. But Joe could sway and roll and you could never land your punches on him—a really hard man to fight. So the score with Joe at that point was 2–2 because as amateurs I'd beaten him twice and lost once.

On February 28, 1956, I fought Maurice Mols, the French champion, at the Albert Hall. That was all over in the fourth round. He was a short, roly-poly sort of fighter, a bit overweight, and I could see I was hurting him just with the straight left. I caught him with a good left hook in the fourth and that was it, a comparatively easy fight. Then on May 1 came Brian London, for the first time. Brian had fought as Brian Harper as an amateur. The son of the former British heavyweight champion, Jack London, Brian to a lot of people was the North of England where I was the South. He'd won the Commonwealth Games heavyweight title at Vancouver in 1954, and since turning professional had won a dozen fights, all but one inside the distance. He was a rough, tough fighter, and there was plenty of room for a bit of blood rivalry. I'd beaten his brother Jack as an amateur, and Brian had beaten George, my brother, in four rounds as a pro. Freddie Mills promoted us at the old Empress Hall, but I wasn't able to do him much of a turn. It was all over in the first round. I caught Brian with a good left hook which more or less propped him up in the corner. I carried on hitting him, which kept him up,; if I'd come away I think he would have just fallen down. As it was he was in no condition to fight on, and the referee came in and pulled me away and stopped it. That first round was remarkable for one of the few good right hands to the body I can remember putting in. I hit Brian with it well enough for him to bring his hands down and he was wide open to the left hook. It was far easier than I thought it would be. Giannino Luise, an Italian I fought next, I'd scarcely heard of before and I heard nothing of him afterwards. He was a great big guy, about fifteen stone, and very strong. In the seventh I caught him with a good punch to the liver which really hurt him and the referee stopped the fight.

Sometimes it's as well you can't see into the future. I would never have guessed after beating Luise so easily on that night of June 26, 1956, that I would have gone seven fights in the next two years with only one win to my name. In the first year I lost four fights in a row from September to September, the blackest year of my boxing life. The following year looks almost as bad from the record books, but it was really a very different story. The bad year began on September 7 at Manchester against Peter Bates. At that point Bates was reckoned a good prospect. He was a big boy, around 15 stone, and I liked big fellows. I was always lightish for a heavyweight, which meant I was a quicker mover, could get in and out, and could miss a lot of the trouble. Big men's reflexes are also that much slower. Peter Bates was one fight I should never have lost. It was the main fight of the evening and in the first round I had him down and the official count was nine, but it was a slow count. It was touch and go whether he beat it, but anyway the ref let him get up, and I was still giving him a towsing when suddenly, wallop! — in the fifth round my eye came open. It was in the same place but a worse cut than the Bacilieri one, and that was it. A setback, I thought, but the luck of the game. I had a good five-month break to get over the cut eye and I then met Joe Bygraves. I'd beaten him fairly easily two years earlier, for the British Empire heavyweight title. This was one of the fights where the only possible explanation for my bad display was weight. It was at Earls Court in London and my first shot at a pro title. I weighed in the heaviest I have ever weighed, 13 stone 13. I couldn't move, I couldn't find any rhythm, yet I'd trained hard in the gym, done everything I should have done except get the weight. In the ninth round Joe caught me with a body shot that winded me. I was down just gasping for breath as I was counted out. It was not that Joe was so good but that I was so bad.

Jim said, 'Well, you've had a bad one. Have a couple of months out of the gym.' So I did, and I came back with a match lined up against Ingemar Johansson in Stockholm on May 19 for the European title. Later, Johansson was to take the world title off Floyd Patterson, but at that time he had fought sixteen fights—two less than me—and had just beaten the Italian, Franco Cavicchi, for the European title. Anyone could lose against Johansson; he had a hell of a right-hand punch. He was also the worst fellow in the world to box. He liked a man to come to him, and we knew it. Our tactics were to make him come after us, make him reverse his usual style. We knew he had a good right-hand counter punch. So for four rounds I'm standing my ground and Johansson's standing his. It was in the open air, and they were crafty. They stuck me in the corner where the sun was shining on my eyes. For four rounds, then, I'm saying to myself, 'I'm not going to take the fight to you.' It was a lousy fight. Johansson would flick with his left hand and that was all. I could hear the crowd getting restless and then start to talk. A hum comes over the arena when everyone's talking. I went back to the corner after the fourth and Jim says, 'We'll have to do something here.' So, like a fool, I take the fight to him, thinking someone's got to make a go of this. What does he do? He backed me up where the sun was in my eyes and bosh!, he gave me a really good right-hand punch. I didn't see it. I got up, but I was groggy and the referee stopped it. I'd been kidded up to a point, but I'd also kidded myself. I let this crowd noise affect my judgment. I should have carried on just as I was, but I was a bit young then, only twenty-three, and I thought someone had to do something.

Johansson was the playboy of heavyweight boxing. He broke all the conventional rules, including training rules. He had a girl friend, Bridget, whom he married afterwards, and she'd be in his training camp. He'd go to night clubs, dancing until midnight. Girls are usually taboo in boxers' training camps. Not with Johansson. Even when he fought Patterson in America he took Bridget with him. She was at his hotel and there would be pictures of them at the swimming pool. He didn't seem to be training too hard and the American critics were knocking him for it, but he still beat Patterson.

To my mind, women and fights—boxing matches, any-way—don't mix because it's simply not practical. With women in training camps it wouldn't be the sex that impaired boxing performance but the building up to it. With most women you've got to have a drink and this, that and the other, and it's the leading up that does you no good, not the physical act of sex. It's been proved that sex in itself doesn't impair athletic performance, but if you're not married you can't expect to have sex at half-past eight and turn over and go straight off to sleep; but in training camp you're up early in the morning and you've got to get to sleep early.

Johansson, though, had his own ideas of training. He wanted to enjoy himself and train as well, which in my opinion is a little bit hard to do. There's an old saying that you can't burn the candle at both ends—not for long, any-way. And in fact Johansson got clobbered once or twice, and I think he was wise to retire when he did. He was pretty wealthy; he'd had some good money fights with Patterson for the world title. And he was quite an idol in Sweden;

he made films, and he was a good-looking boy. He modelled clothes and did lots of advertising. Also he had good investments. He had roadbuilding machines, earth-movers and bulldozers, and seemed to end up OK.

I took another four-month break, then on September 17 it was Joe Erskine for the fifth time—but on this occasion for the British title. I still hadn't learned my lesson. I boxed quite well and it was close enough for me to think I might have got the verdict. But it went to Joe, and again I'd made the mistake of letting him get into his stride and letting his old poker face set me wondering whether I'd hurt him or not. He'd kidded me long enough though. Whenever we fought again I would go out and hurt him in the first round, and be the governor right from the start. Of course our rivalry was built up as the biggest thing in British boxing, but we got on well personally. I think we had a lot of respect for each other. I suppose the relationships between boxers, between people who do violence to each other one moment then pay them a compliment the next, must puzzle some people. I've never hit anyone in real anger outside the ring. Inside, if you do hit them with anger, it has to be controlled. You like or dislike people the same as everyone else. Joe I liked. Brian London was one I didn't like in the early years, though it was different later, when I used to send him a good luck telegram before a fight and he would do the same for me. But in the early years he seemed a miserable so-and-so, a surly bloke, never smiling in his pictures and a difficult man to get along with. Not that he'd ever really done anything to me. But from his attitude when we met at weigh-ins there was no love lost between us. He could be quick-tempered in the ring, too. He'd sling a punch on the bell, and I'd come back at him—little things. In later years we got on much better. Usually you will send a telegram to someone you know a bit, especially if they've sent one to you. After I'd beaten London a couple of times he said something which made me laugh. 'Henry so loves me he's got me over his mantelpiece.' And after the third time, 'Well, I'm Henry's now,' which was a reference to the fact that if you win a British heavyweight title fight three times you win a Lonsdale belt. The climate changed with that sort of thing.

But that was still in the future. There was me in the

autumn of 1957, beaten by Bates, Bygraves, Johansson and Erskine in succession, and we didn't know what was going wrong. That was the nearest I came to retiring from boxing. We were doing everything we should have done in the ring. I was training hard. I wasn't gallivanting around enjoying myself. My whole life was boxing. I was still living at home, I was looking good in the gym, but nothing was going right in the ring. And I was getting despondent. I was worrying about the two cut eyes in the fights with Bacilieri and Bates and about other fights where I was getting little nicks. Jim said, 'Look, son, if you don't relax and leave the cuts to us you might as well get out of the game. Go away, have a rest and think about it.' So I went away and had a think, and then I told Jim, 'I'm looking good in the gym, I'm training well, let's go on a bit longer.' George was still having trouble with his eyes, and we had been getting a bit down together. In January 1956 he lost on a cut eye, and in February at the Albert Hall he lost in the same way. Then in November 1956 at the Granby Halls, Leicester, again it was a cut eye. On my bill in Stockholm, when I fought Ingemar Johansson, George was disqualified in the seventh round against another British fighter, Albert Finch. And in September he was stopped, again with a cut eye, against Manuel Burgo, a big coloured fellow. So it was a really dodgy time. Mum never interfered, but she sensed our depression. Dad, of course, was choked with the rest of us. But while Mum and Dad always encouraged us, they never said you should be doing this or the other.

My stock in my own country was worth nothing. Promoters didn't want to use me. So Jim said the best thing we could do was try for one or two fights on the Continent and get our confidence back. Then in Britain they might want us again. So that's what we did. We went out and had a fight with Hans Kalbfell in Dortmund on November 16, 1957, and although I say it myself I boxed brilliantly. At that time it was the best performance of my life. He was the German champion, a big fellow, about sixteen pounds heavier than me. I was 13 stone 6, he was 6 feet 4, and we had a hell of a battle. I had one or two nicks round my eyes but it didn't bother me. I outboxed him completely, and when the decision was announced the German crowd picked me up and walked me all round the hall shouting 'Wunderbar! Wunderbar.' It was marvellous.

When we came home promoters started showing interest again. Jim then pulled one of the best publicity stunts of his life. He gave out the story that we'd been to a German professor who was teaching me how to relax—Jim was at it long before the Beatles! Henry had met this professor, so he said, and the therapy was working a treat. The papers lapped it up, and it was great. In fact the 'Professor' was a nice little German girl called Hilda. I wasn't married or courting at that time, and she was my relaxing therapy. She was introduced to me at the hotel where we were staying, and after the fight I took her out a few times and then went back for a holiday when I saw her again. I also met her when I went out to fight Heinz Neuhaus in Dortmund on January 11, 1958. We got a draw there, and it was the hardest draw I ever got, because I won nine rounds out of ten—and giving him one round is generous. Afterwards they said, 'Oh yeah, but you didn't win by five clear points.' We thought, well, what a liberty! But there again, the crowd enjoyed it. They have a different points system on the Continent, of course, using whole numbers with a maximum of five per round. But they made no secret that any foreign boxer had to win by five clear points before he got the decision.

When you go abroad you have to expect home town refereeing. Foreigners coming to this country get the best crack of all because our referees bend over backwards to be fair. But not so in Germany and Italy. You've got very partisan crowds and the referees often are affected by it. But the hardest part was to come. For my third successive fight in Germany I was lined up against Erich Schoeppner, their light-heavyweight champion, in Frankfurt. They said Schoeppner was a great draw and they were building him up to fight Archie Moore, the world light-heavyweight champion at the time. Jim thought they were mad to match him with me. 'If you want to keep him a crowd draw why match him with Cooper?' Jim asked. 'Oh no,' the promoter said. 'He'll give Cooper a good fight.' 'Cooper will knock him out,' Jim said. He'd watched Schoeppner fight Arthur Howard when I'd previously fought in Germany. But the Germans badly wanted the fight and we made it for April 19, 1958. Schoeppner, being a light-heavy, was a little faster for two or three rounds. He was a bit flashy, but pretty useful, and in those first rounds, probably just edging it. But I thought, 'He's shooting his bolt here. He won't be able to last this for any distance.' In the fourth and fifth rounds he was getting tired, and I came on a bundle. In the sixth round I'm belting him. I pushed him on to the ropes with a left hand and as he came off he turned away, in exhaustion and tiredness, I think. But my punch, a left hook, was on the way, and it hit him on the ear and he went down spark out. It took him a hell of a time to recover; in fact they had to carry him out the ring on a stretcher. He was in hospital for about five weeks afterwards. But going back to the fight, the referee had counted him out. I thought I'd won and we were all happy and chatty in the corner. Then suddenly over the loudspeaker system there's this German voice rhubarbing away and the crowd is going potty. 'What's all this?' says Jim to Jean Brutnel, a Frenchman who's going in next, and who speaks good English. He says to Jim, 'They've taken a liberty with you.' I'm joking. I say, 'What, have they given us the draw again?' He says, 'No, they've disqualified you.' They didn't give any explanation. I said, 'What a liberty! The guy turned into me. He was turning himself and the punch was on the way—it couldn't be helped.' But they'd disqualified me all right—for rabbit punching—and they also stopped £700, half my purse. We found out afterwards that the German Boxing Federation was pretty well bankrupt and they could only pay one fight bill from the proceeds of the earlier one. Henry Cooper gave them a bit of a helping hand, but Henry Cooper never fought in Germany again.

People in England read about these fights, but there weren't as many television sets in those days, and most couldn't tell for themselves how I was doing. But I knew those three fights had restored my self-confidence. A lot of people put the Dick Richardson fight, the one at Porthcawl on September 3, as the turning point. In many ways it was. But I'd learned to live with myself, with the fact of nicked eyes, in those three fights in Germany. At Porthcawl most people expected Richardson to win. He was a rough, tough kid, and it was expected he would cut my eye and it would be all over. But as far as British fans were concerned, this was my comeback. Not that everything went smoothly. The fight had to be postponed a week because my own brother cut my eye in the ring. It was the silliest of accidents. Jim had got hold of a coloured sparring partner who was supposed to be able to take a punch. When it came to it I knocked him out in two punches, so Jim told George, who was all geared up, to go in and finish the round. George, with the inside of his glove, cut my eye. Teddy Waltham, Secretary of the Board, was there, and there was nothing for it but to postpone the fight. Fortunately the eye healed quickly. I knew Dick Richardson in the Army, and I'm sure he won't mind me saying he was a better fighter on the cobbles than he ever was in the ring. He'd be a hell of a good friend in a rough-house. At Aldershot, when he was in the Service Corps, and we were in the Ordnance, he used to terrorise the place. He'd lost to George in their first pro fight, but now he was on his way up. Let's face it, Dick could be a rough fighter, but I knew him and was prepared for it. Dick realised that very few referees were strong enough to disqualify a man in the first round. He was a rugger player and I'm sure he used to think he was back in those scrums. He would come in there fighting with his head down, bom, bom, bom! I was ready for him, yet still he did me! He came out in the first round, cracked me with the nut, bop!, and my eyebrow was split to the middle of my forehead. It really was one that went up vertically. So, naturally, I had a little swear at him, 'You so-and-so,' because I'd known he was going to try it. But then we got down to the boxing, and it see-sawed up and down until in the fifth round he put me down. He only shook me, he didn't have me groggy, and the film shows that I'm only on my haunches. I looked at my corner and mouthed at them 'I'm all right, don't worry.' But Dick thought I was in bad trouble and came smashing in like a bull in a china shop, his guard well down. Then, wallop! — I caught him with a peach of a left hook. It took him off his feet about six inches, and down he stayed. He was well out, big fellow that he was; that was one of the best punches I ever landed.

Once again I'd been cut, but Danny Holland did a good job on it, and never again did I worry about cuts to the extent that they affected my performance. I had learned to live with them. I had also set myself up in Britain once more and the promoters were talking our terms again. They needed to, after that postponement, for keeping on sparring partners and all the other extra expenses cost us an additional £1,500. We only got £6,000 all told, and everything had to come out of that.

CHAPTER EIGHT

In October 1958 there was a major breakthrough when for the first time I was matched not simply with a top American but one of the world's top three, Zora Folley. It came about in a very unlikely way. Jim had fixed a fight with the Argentinian, Alex Miteff, but at six o'clock one morning he was woken up by a phone call from New York from Bill Daly. 'I've got some bad news for you,' Bill said. Jim was only half awake. 'What's that?' he said. 'Miteff won't be able to fight,' Bill told him. 'That's no bad news for us,' Jim said, 'that's bad news for Harry Levene.' Harry was promoting us. Miteff had broken a bone in his leg while fighting Willie Besmanoff. 'Anyway, thanks for calling us,' Jim said. He then called Levene's agent, Bobby Diamond, because Harry is a strict Jew, this was Passover, and he was at the synagogue.

Next day Jim and Harry got together and looked over the leading ten fighters in Nat Fleischer's *Ring Magazine*. Co-top were Zora Folley and Archie Moore; Patterson was champion at the time. At the bottom was a man named Sonny Liston. Some time before, Jim Norris of the World Boxing Association had been with Jim, backing a few horses in Jack Solomons's office. Conversationally Norris had said to Jim : 'If you're offered a guy called Sonny Liston, don't have him.' In boxing parlance Liston was reckoned an 'animal'. In other words a big, rough, tough fighter who was none too fussy. Meantime Harry had asked an American contact to get hold of Liston. Chris Dundee, who was promoting a Liston fight in California, was ready to release him to Levene, but Jim didn't know that as they sat down. Levene said : 'Who shall we take?' Jim answered : 'I'll take anyone out of the first ten except Valdez and Liston.' He barred Nino Valdez, the Cuban, because he was a good fighter, but big and awkward, and Jim believed in picking and choosing. 'If the boys won a fight and a good purse without getting touched, then I'd done my job,' Jim would say. Harry was surprised, though he didn't let on he'd more or less made the match. That came out afterwards. 'I don't know who Liston is,' Jim said, 'but I don't want him.' 'You'll take the top two then?' asked Harry. 'Yeah,' said Jim. Jim knew he wouldn't get Archie Moore for the amount of money that could be offered. To Jim's surprise, though, Zora Folley took us up. Folley was a good box-fighter who could punch. Usually you're a puncher or a boxer. When you can combine both, then you are a hell of a hard fellow to beat.

The fight was my first at Wembley Pool. For the first three rounds Folley outjabbed me, and caught me well, and most people were saying, 'That's all over.' I had one or two cuts on the face, and when he put me down in the third round I didn't have a price. But it was then that he made his big mistake. When I got up he went right-hand crazy. He forgot his boxing and he just wanted to stop me by throwing right hands. He let me in, because if he'd carried on boxing he would perhaps have beaten me; I say perhaps because you can never be completely sure, no matter how much one man seems to be on top. But all the while he was setting himself up for those big right hands I had my old trombone left working. I came back into the fight, and in the end won it, and well won it. It gave me a marvellous boost because I knew then that I could beat a man in the very highest world class.

I suppose Folley took the fight because they thought it would be an easy pay day—they couldn't have been getting more than a couple of thousand pounds. There are one or two myths about American boxing. Boxers from the States often took peanuts compared with the money Jim would let me fight for abroad. He'd laugh at a promoter offering us two thousand pounds to fight Folley. A lot of people believe that in America there are millions of dollars to be earned, but it's a misconception. There is for the world heavyweight champion, and for one or two top contenders. But that's all. Boxers in the lower weights have to fight all over the Americas to make some money.

How to assess your opposition, whether you take it or not,

then how you go into the fight is a highly individual matter. I've never been a great one for studying fight films; I'd perhaps have been a better fighter if I had. I might watch once, but not base tactics on it. I never believed in going in the ring with a set plan. Fighters react differently to different opponents. Against one fighter my style might be completely different to the guy who'd fought him in the film I'd been watching, and he wouldn't do what I was expecting. I'd then have to sling my plan out of the window. I've always believed boxing to be an ad lib game. You take a fight as it reveals itself in front of you. Your sensible planning for a man like Folley would be to find out whether he was a right-hand puncher or a left-hooker. Jim would phone up friends or contacts in America, people like Jimmy Fragetti, an agent, or Bill Daly, who managed Manuel Ortiz and Lee Savold, and exchange information, especially if a man was not in the record books. Then you could check on the *Ring Annual*'s records and ratings. At its simplest, if a man wins ninety per cent of his fights on points then you know he's a boxer. If another guy wins ninety per cent inside the distance you know he's a puncher—and you may want to avoid him! And there are those in between who, equally, you assess with the help of a tip or two, and by working out whom he beat and when.

After Folley we could concentrate on our No. 1 target— the British and Empire heavyweight titles. Brian London had taken them off Joe Erskine in the middle of 1958 when he'd knocked him out in the seventh round. On January 12, 1959, I met Brian at Earls Court for one of the hardest fights I ever had. I felt worse after this, more exhausted, and in more pain, than with any other. From the first round I had a nose bleed at the very top of the nostril. It wasn't so much running down my nose as down the back of my throat. That meant I was swallowing blood for the whole fifteen rounds. I also had one or two nasty cuts underneath the eye. The only good thing about it was that the blood didn't run into the eye and affect my vision. All the same, I outboxed him, jabbing him silly, and I say silly because at the end of the fourteenth Brian stuck up my hand thinking it was the last round—he didn't realise he still had another round to go! We were both badly marked—he had bruises and fat eyes—but one or two good judges made me ahead by

$3\frac{3}{4}$ points at the finish. There I was then, British champion for the first time, and I was to stay so until Joe Bugner beat me just over twelve years later, though there was a short period when I turned the title in on a matter of principle.

There's not much chance of getting a fat head in this game. I still had plenty of critics. Some said I looked too apprehensive in the ring, others that I was too rigid. I think this was a fair comment, but after the German fights and Folley and London, I began to relax. I didn't worry so much. When I had a cut I didn't even ask Danny how it was. I just let him work on it. Before that I would ask anxiously, 'Is it bad? Will they stop it?' I was trying too hard, and tensing up, which is tiring enough in itself besides the damage the other fellow is doing to you.

I had a good long break, and then, on August 26, 1959, I defended my Empire title against the South African, Gawie de Klerk, a Johannesburg policeman, at Porthcawl. Coney Beach where we fought really was a dump. The dressing-rooms were made of corrugated iron. This was August, it was a nice day, and it was stinking hot. Some time after, Coney Beach was burned down, to no sorrow of mine, and they now have a new arena which is very nice, but I didn't get the benefit of it. On the other hand the crowd could not be fairer. Welsh crowds know their boxing. They're aficionados just as the Spanish are with their bull fights. Most in the crowd have probably done a bit of boxing. I'm an Englishman, but against de Klerk I was their boy. Even against Dick Richardson, as Welsh as they come, they'd still be very fair with you. De Klerk was pretty rugged, a young strong fellow, and there wasn't much in it in the first three rounds. Then I caught him with a series of good punches, he was out on his feet, and the referee stopped the fight.

But on November 17, 1961, at Earls Court came the real test of my confidence. Here I was up against Joe Erskine for the sixth time. He'd beaten me twice as a professional, something no one else had done, and if anyone qualified as a bogyman it was Joe. But now I was meeting him as the champion and I didn't give him any chance. I went straight out after him from the first bell. This was the occasion when he went over the bottom rope and I've never seen a man balance there like it. That really had me scared. I was pleased to see him come to. I thought his back was broken. Jim was pleased, too; he was in the corner shivering. We had an affection for Joe, as I've said. Whenever accidents happen in the ring it's usually because a man falls awkwardly. With Joe in this fight I caught him with some really heavy punches. He'd been down once before, but then I caught him with two combination punches, left-right, left-right, and, as he was going down, with another left hook. That's when things happen. It's when they fall awkwardly, or hit their heads awkwardly as they fall, that you get these serious injuries and fatalities in boxing.

I was twenty-seven then and the left hook was at its peak. I was taking them out with one punch and the timing was exactly right. Most British heavyweights have been boxers rather than punchers. Just before me Johnny Williams was certainly one of these. Jack Gardner was a big fellow but he didn't really have a big punch. Tommy Farr was a boxer, not a puncher. It's hard to give a reason why we haven't produced bigger punchers. Punchers are born, not made. You don't really develop a puncher. He might improve his big punch but he's got it there, at the start. You don't get boxers who suddenly turn into punchers. A punch has little to do with muscles; it's a matter of reflexes and timing. Jimmy Wilde never went more than 7 stone 5 and he was as thin as a matchstick, but he could knock out welter-weights. In boxing a punching muscle is a long, not a bunched muscle, such as a weightlifter gets. All good punchers have the knack of meeting a man as he's coming on to the punch which doubles the effectiveness with the two sets of weights then involved. It's like the head-on car crash as opposed to the one where the car hits something which gives. Both can be nasty but one a lot nastier than the other. Good punches never travel more than nine inches. That still gets all the body weight behind it. Some people are hard long punchers but the really outstanding ones make it short and sharp. Some research was done on me by a scientific team from the RAF's Institute of Aviation Medicine. Flight Lieutenant Dick Borland, a bio-physicist, analysed 6,600 pictures taken by a camera in six seconds. My left fist's acceleration over five and a half inches was found to equal sixty times the force of gravity. At the end of the five and a half inches the fist was travelling at 30 mph with the whole body weight behind it. The punch, he said, lasted only forty-eight thousandths of a second and even when they slowed it down more than forty times it was still too fast for the eye to see. They projected eighty frames, one by one, and they were able to measure the distance the fist travelled every five frames. So that was Enery's 'ammer as the camera saw it, or didn't see it.

As champion you live in the best room in the house, so to speak. You've gone from the kitchen to the dining-room to the drawing-room—and some would call it the lounge judging by the number of fights you take! I fought only twice in 1960, twice in 1961, three times in 1962, twice in 1963, and twice in 1964. As far as the public is concerned, that's about five hours work in five years—lovely grub, they think. But it doesn't really operate like that.

The tax situation hits you straight away. The majority of boxers, and I'm talking of those who reach the top, earn good money for five years, top whack. I was an exception. Jim and me fought strongly to get the tax situation changed so that a fighter would get the same treatment as an author, with tax deductions spread over a period of years. Right at the end of my career, when there was no advantage to be gained for me personally, we were still campaigning for this on a straightforward matter of principle. One year we earned £36,000 and out of that the taxman took £29,000. That left £7,000, which is not much when you have to keep up appearances and move and spend money in a different circle from what you were doing as a plasterer. Jim would never take a penny expenses from a charity organisation we might be helping, though often they suggested it. A Labour MP, Tam Dalyell, once put the spreadover of sportsmen's tax in a private member's Bill, and Jim and me were in the gallery at the House of Commons hoping he would get a chance. But Denis Howell, the Minister for Sport then, came up to tell us there would be no more time and the question never came up. I think there's a fair amount of goodwill to the idea on both sides of the House—Eldon Griffiths, the Conservative Minister for Sport, is on our side for one—and with a bit of luck it will go through one day. But I had a situation where, after expenses and the usual allowances, I was paying the taxman 16s. 9d. on every pound I earned. People said why don't you fight more. My answer was why don't you try getting punched on the nose for nothing !

The ideal was three or four fights a year. I was never one who wanted to box seven or eight times, not as champion, anyway. I lasted so long because I was never overboxed. All fighters have only so many fights in them; you can have them all quick or space them out. There were plenty of fighters around. Some people said why don't you take less money and fight them a bit more. But it's a basic point of business with everyone; you want to get the most you can for the job you do. Once you go in cheap for one promoter you've got to do it all the time. If I went in for £5,000 for Jack Solomons I couldn't turn round and ask for ten grand from Harry Levene. It's their business to get me as cheap as they can in the early years. It's my business to sell myself as dearly as possible as champion. Jim still had a stable of fighters at this time. He had boxers like Vic Andreetti, Kenny Field and Billy Davies, but the strain told on him after a while. He wasn't getting any younger—he was sixty when we had our first professional fight—and the tax man started to worry the life out of him. By the middle 1960s he was only looking after George and me. He couldn't face any longer the two jobs of keeping records of expenses and income and handling fighters. The breaking point came, I think, when *Boxing News* printed the wrong date for a fight involving Alex Buxton and Albert Finch. Jim gave the tax people the right date but they had him on the carpet to explain why he hadn't entered figures for the two fights. They had no idea that under Boxing Board of Control regulations you couldn't fight on successive days.

While some things changed drastically for me as the new champion, others stayed much the same. We still lived in the same council house, we still ate much the same food. More people wanted to use you; not just promoters but press and television, wanting your views on fights and so on, and publicity agents wanting you to open a supermarket or a shop; that sort of thing. I would usually put them on to Jim if they approached me directly. I left all money and appointment matters for him to sift through. Then he'd get on the phone and discuss things with me. That wasn't quite as easy as it seems. We weren't on the telephone at Bellingham and Jim would sometimes send me a telegram to call him immediately. We would get this at half-past eight in the morning. So off I'd go to the local telephone box. I'd go in the booth . . . Jim would be engaged. Ten minutes, half an hour . . . still engaged. Then someone would come up wanting to use the box. I'd have to go outside and pace around. Then I'd go off to another box. Still engaged. At times Jim would be talking for an hour. And directly I got on to him, before I'd opened my mouth, he'd be at me: 'Where have you been? I told you to ring.' Jim is the greatest telephone talker in the world. When he had a big stable doing a lot of business a telephone bill of £170 to £200 was nothing for him. One call and the right horse and he'd have that back, of course!

We were perfectly happy at home. Mum always looked after us well. We knew our diet—before a fight, for example, it was only a salad and a steak. We had always spent plenty of money on food, even if it meant we had little for anything else. I'm quite a small eater; I prefer to eat little and often rather than sit down and gorge course after course. When I was in serious training before a big fight I'd eat less than ever. At that time I'd reckon three weeks of strict training for a big fight. In later years, as I grew older, I would need a little longer to get to a peak and I would give myself five weeks.

We had several training camps over the twelve years I was British champion. The Bull's Head in Chislehurst was the chief place for many years, but when the people there retired we moved to the Clive Hotel, Hampstead, and trained at the Noble Art gym on Haverstock Hill. We had the same routine throughout. We'd get up at quarter to four in the morning, have a quick wash, clean our teeth, slip into track suits and heavy boots—I always believed in Army boots—and be on the road by 4 am. We'd then do forty minutes of running and exercises along the road, which represented about four or five miles of road work. I was never a long-distance man. Sometimes you hear of boxers running seven to ten miles. I don't believe in that. There is such a thing as leaving your form on the road or in the gym. We'd have no rest, keeping on the move all the time. Road work is the worst part for any boxer. I'd much sooner have gone in the ring and sparred. When you're not fit it's hard on the legs and wind, and your lungs feel they are going to burst, but you can't ease up. And it never gets easy. The fitter you get the harder you push yourself. You were just as tired after a day's work in the second week of training as you were on the first day. After a forty-five minute run we'd rest and sweat out. Boxers don't run like athletes at Meadowbank or the Crystal Palace, just in singlets and shorts. We run not only with heavy boots but in track suits with one or two thick sweaters underneath. We would need to sweat out for ten minutes to a quarter of an hour, and then we would jump in the bath and have a good wash. After that my brother would give me a good spirit rub using a cheap cologne, which closes the pores — then back into bed and sleep. I had no problems with sleeping. Hard physical exercise is better than any sleeping pill for knocking you out. You don't lie there worrying about the day. Your head hits the pillow and within two or three minutes you're asleep. We would get up again at 8.30, wash, shave, dress and go down to breakfast. I would always eat a light breakfast — George would usually want more — of half a grapefruit with sugar, one poached or boiled egg (never a fry-up because I didn't fancy fatty stuff), a couple of slices of toast and marmalade, and three or four cups of lemon tea or coffee. I was always more thirsty than hungry after a run and all the sweating. After that we would go for a gentle walk to pass the time, then come back, sit in the lounge and read the newspapers until about one o'clock, when we would go into the gym for training. I didn't feel so cut off from the world that I didn't want to read the papers, but I would always read from the back to the front. It was all the sport first, then the entertainment pages to see what was on telly that night, and then up into the general news. I wouldn't be thinking about boxing all the time. I could relax and forget about it completely until it was time to go to the gym.

There our work would vary depending whether we were in the early or late stages of training. You would build up gradually to ten or twelve rounds — a couple of rounds of shadow boxing just to warm up, then a couple of rounds of the heavy bag, two or three rounds of skipping, a couple of rounds on the speed ball, then twenty to twenty-five minutes of ground work, which was exercising with the medicine ball, toning stomach muscles up, and light weight-lifting. I don't believe in too much weight-lifting for boxers. It bunches and knots those long boxing muscles and you lose elasticity. After this we would sweat out again, shower, and George would give me another spirit rub. That way we never caught colds, although it would have been easy enough to do so in the winter when we came out of a hot gym. We would be back to the hotel at about 2 or 2.30 and eat our main meal of the day. I'd usually have a slice of melon or some smoked salmon, perhaps a trout, then steak, medium done, and a mixed salad. In the early days of training I would switch it around a bit; pork one day, chicken the next, beef the next, but later on, nearer the fight day, I would stick to steak, medium done, and then finish off with cheese or ice-cream, and a couple of cups of coffee. I would always have a couple of glasses of red wine; Jim encouraged us to do that, and I always enjoyed it. Afterwards we would have very little. About six o'clock it would be a cup of tea, toast and a few biscuits, and that was all until the next morning's breakfast. After I was married I would always phone Albina at about seven, just before Henry—and later John as well—went to bed, so that I could have a talk with them on the phone. We'd watch television for a couple of hours, then be in bed sharp at 9.30. Once again, sleep was no problem. Even on the eve of a big fight I would never lie in bed worrying and wondering.

CHAPTER NINE

In January 1960 my life changed in the most dramatic way possible short of me giving up boxing. I married Albina, then twenty-three, but whom I'd known since she was a sixteen-year-old girl serving us in Peter Mario's restaurant, in London's Gerrard Street, just off Shaftesbury Avenue. The life of a boxer has a good many routines, and one which Jim Wicks and I had shared for years was to eat in certain restaurants on certain days—sometimes we'd even break training camp to do it. It suited our relationship, our business lives, and our liking for particular sorts of food. Usually on Mondays, or the early part of the week, we would go to Simpson's in the Strand because we were especially fond of the roast duck, saddle of mutton, or roast beef cut from the joint on the trolley. Around the middle of the week it would be Peter Mario's. I love veal escalope Milanaise and spaghetti Bolognaise, and George and me had discovered this place years before. On Fridays it would be Sheekey's fish restaurant in St Martin's Court, just off the Charing Cross Road, with oysters, a main fish course and a bottle of Krug Champagne, or No 7 on the wine card. The point is that certain restaurants are famous for certain things, and after a while everyone knows you and makes a fuss of you. Let's face it, you're a good customer and they make a little more of you perhaps than a guy who comes in once every two or three months. It's nice because you get to know all the people there and I enjoy that sort of personal treatment.

Peter Mario's was started by a partnership of Peter Rizzi, Albina's uncle, and a man called Mario. When Mario left they decided to keep the name the same. Aunt Maria, Peter Rizzi's wife, had the idea in 1948 of bringing Albina over. Aunt Maria was Albina's father's sister. She and Uncle Peter were in fact born in England, and they knew that Albina's family were having a hard time on their little farm. Well, farm, it's more a smallholding at a little village called Boccacci, near Parma in the foothills of the Apennines. Aunt Maria said to Albina's Mum, 'Send her over to us and she'll get a nice education and she can work in the shop.' Albina's mother, another Maria—her father is Giuseppe—was taken with the idea, and so was Albina, who hated farm life. She's not an animal lover and much preferred to work inside rather than outside the house, even as a child. She fed the chickens and collected the eggs, but she would never go near the barn to help her mother feed the cows—they petrified her.

The people there live a very hard life. Albina's mother works harder than almost any man I know. I was a plasterer, but her mother's hands were a lot harder than mine even when I was working in the building trade. They have a lot of heavy manual work to do, so naturally that was another reason for trying to find Albina something different. She's only a little woman now, and at ten she was less than half her present height. Farming in that part of Italy can't really be compared with farming here at home. Her Dad has two fields in one place and another a mile away. A half-mile farther on and he's got another. They've a couple of cows, a few sheep and chickens, and a couple of pigs. They grow their own wheat and oats and literally live off the land. The milkman will come mornings and evenings after they have milked the cows. They have a book in which they weigh and enter the amounts and at the right time of the year, say in June, they will get back so much cheese. If there is anything over they might then get a bit of money back, but almost everything is done on the bartering principle. They grow their own wheat, have it threshed, then the baker takes it away and provides them with bread all through the year. They don't send what they produce to co-operatives or export anything; they're not that big. They don't even grow or fatten stuff for the towns. They live off the land in the strictest sense.

In 1948, too, Italy was only gradually recovering from the war. Albina was born in 1937 so she was very young when most of the fighting was going on farther south. She didn't realise the seriousness of it all, but they would all be very frightened when the soldiers came down into the village. She has two brothers and a sister, all of them younger, and the last, Giovanni, was not born when the soldiers came to take her father away along with other men of the village. Why they were going no one knew. The three children and their mother followed them down the track and as far as the road, crying all the while. Suddenly the soldiers—they were Italians, not Germans—let her father go, and he ran back from the road to them. Perhaps it was because of the children's tears; no one will ever know. But father's still there on his farm, and we visit them every year in late July and August.

When the bombers flew low they would run into the fields and hide, but their other big adventure was when the village sheltered two escaping British soldiers. Everyone helped out. Most of them were pretty pro-British in any case, but Albina's family were especially so with Uncle Peter and Aunt Maria living in England. By then, too, Italy was formally on the British side. Even so, it was a pretty dangerous thing to do with the Germans or Fascist soldiers shooting anyone who helped the British or Americans. There was one soldier—his name was Peter and he was a captain—who was in Albina's father's house one particular morning when her mother and father got the word that the soldiers were coming to search for Englishmen. Giuseppe had a chimney hidden by a wooden bench in one of his rooms, and he told Peter to get in there. The soldiers searched the four bedrooms, the stables, and the cantina, or cellar, all the most likely places where they might find fugitives, but they didn't discover the chimney. Many years later, it must have been 1967, Peter came back to visit the family and see all the people of the village. He could only speak a few words of Italian, but he never forgot them.

Although she was so young when she came to England Albina felt quite happy about it. Although she had never met either her uncle or aunt, she knew she was going to join family. She was sent to the Notre Dame de France school in Leicester Square, and then to St Peter's and Paul's School in Amwell Street in Clerkenwell. After leaving at fifteen she was sent on a dressmaking course, but she hated it. Aunt Maria finally said, 'Well, you can come and work in the restaurant like we do.' So Albina started as a waitress, and began to send home bits and pieces of money to her parents. Eventually, both her brothers and her sister joined her here. Both brothers are chefs and her sister is married to an Italian waiter.

Albina was only sixteen when I first remember her at the restaurant. I wasn't particularly free and easy with girls. I couldn't usually chat them up. There had been one or two girl friends, but nothing serious, and I had simply taken them out a couple of times and forgotten all about it. But as time went by I found myself chatting more and more to Albina. It sometimes seemed more a brother and sister relationship in that we seemed to have known each other for so long. But I was attracted to her and she was easy to talk to. Asking her for our first date was quite another story. One day during the week, I said: 'Are you working Saturday? Would you like to see a film?' She said: 'Oh yes,' so I said: 'Lovely—see you Saturday.' Well, like a fool, I got all dressed up and went into the restaurant at about seven o'clock. I could see Albina working, but I thought 'She's going to stop in a minute and get ready.' I knew they had a changing-room in the restaurant. So I'm waiting there and at half-past seven to quarter to eight she's still working. Eventually I said to her: 'When are you getting ready?'

She said : 'Getting ready for what?' I said : 'Getting ready to see a film.' She said : 'Oh dear! You meant it.' Then she was all apologies. 'I thought you were joking. I'm sorry, but I'm working.' I went out all embarrassed, thinking 'This is a right muck-up,' and I went to the pictures on my own.

Albina tells a slightly different story. She thought I was taking the mickey. It wasn't the way she thought it should be. 'It's always the woman that chases the man, but I thought to myself I wouldn't stand a chance,' she said to me afterwards, at the risk of making me big-headed. 'I honestly and truly never thought you would turn up.' When she saw me skulking at the back of the restaurant she thought I was waiting for somebody else. She says she even said to me, 'Would you like a cup of coffee while you're waiting?' without realising I was waiting for her. And it didn't dawn on me that she hadn't realised!

It was another three or four weeks before we saw each other again. Albina always says she was the one who suffered most in that time because I was so busy. I can't help feeling I was the fool for not realising that Saturday night was about the worst night you could ask out a girl who worked in a busy restaurant. We started to see each other regularly on her night off earlier in the week, and after about a year we decided to get married. It wasn't one of those affairs where anyone said anything. If people ask : 'When did you actually pop the question?' I can't answer. Nowadays I don't think men do get down on their knees and say : 'Will you marry me, darling?'—if they ever did. We just mutually agreed on a date, and decided it would have to be quiet. I was a bit in the public eye at the time and we didn't want to be mobbed. So we married at St Peter's and Paul's—the church of Albina's old school—with George best man and only about fifty guests, all family and close friends. Father Meyer, a marvellous man, performed the ceremony. He had given me instructions in becoming a Roman Catholic—of course all Albina's relations were strictly Catholic. I hadn't seriously thought about religion before. Although we went to Sunday School, it was basically to keep us off the road and give us somewhere to go on Sunday when everything else was closed. The Catholic doctrines I found easy to accept. There were no violent objections from my mother and father. Actually my father, though he was Church of

England, was christened in St George's Cathedral, Southwark, which is Catholic. And my grandfather had Irish Catholic ancestors. Mum and Dad got on well with Albina straight away, and they knew I wanted to please her by changing. They said, 'All right, if that's what you want to do then you go ahead.'

Every year we look forward to our visit to Italy. We spend about three weeks with the family and another week or so at different Italian resorts. We spent our honeymoon in Diano Marina on the Italian Riviera, and each year we try and visit a different place with the children. Our favourite places are Paraggi, between Portofino and Santa Margharita (where we have sometimes seen Rex Harrison), Calabri, Reggio Amalfi and Cesanatica, but I don't like to go back to the same resort year in, year out. I always look forward, though, to the three weeks at Boccacci.

Henry Marco was born on November 19, 1960, and we had a high old time thinking up various names. In the end we settled on Marco, Albina's grandfather's name, to mark the Italian connection. Both Henry Marco and John Pietro, who was born on August 5, 1967, like the animals on their grandparents' farm a bit more than their mother did, the rabbits especially. Now, too, you begin to see tractors around and they love messing about on those. We've a language problem, up to a point, because Albina's parents speak no English at all, and as for me, although I know hundreds of words of Italian I can't put them together. I never mastered English grammar as a kid so I don't know how I can do it with Italian now. One thing, the mother-in-law never nags me. In fact Albina says she spoils me rotten. She's marvellous! If I call 'Albina!' like I do at home, and Albina doesn't answer in five or ten seconds her Mum says straightaway, 'Albina, Henry's called you and you haven't answered!' And that ends up with Albina having a row with both her mother and me. 'I'm not his servant!' she says. Albina often tells her father off for not even knowing where his hanky is, but really it's her mother who's responsible. If her Dad is getting ready to go anywhere it's her Mum who cleans his shoes, lays his shirt out, lays his suit out, lays his hanky out, lays everything out. Everything has to be ready for him. She even cleans his shoes! Her Dad's never cleaned a pair of boots or shoes in his life. I won't let Albina clean my shoes. I've always had to clean my own. But her Dad's only to say one thing and her Mum will answer and do it. But if I call Albina and Albina doesn't answer up smartly, her Mum is soon rattling away in Italian, 'Henry's calling . . . go on, answer him quickly.' I say : 'Quite right, mother. That's right!' And when Albina gets mad, her mother stage-whispers to her, 'You terrible girl, he's such a good man!' Like Victorian England, the man there is still lord and master.

We bought our house in Wembley soon after returning from our honeymoon. We stayed with Albina's cousin for a couple of months while we were arranging things. The house we chose is almost within sight and sound of Wembley Stadium, but there's really no connection. We started looking there because Albina had relations that side of London. We saw an advert in the *Evening Standard*, visited the place, and liked it at once. It was a nice house in a nice position, with fields at the back and no one overlooking you. It was basically only a three-bedroom house, but after about five years we had a lounge built on with an extra bedroom and bathroom upstairs. We needed room when John was born in 1967. We had to have gates put on outside because people started to poke around the house, peering through the letter box and that sort of thing. It hasn't happened often. People on the whole are pretty good. We get some, especially kids, knocking on our door wanting photographs or autographs, but that's all part of the game. You've got to expect and accept that. It hasn't happened often enough to get on our nerves.

Of course I knew from the word go that Albina didn't like boxing. She didn't understand it, she was scared that I would get hurt, but she accepted that it was my work. She doesn't know any other boxer's wife, and socially we don't mix in a boxing circle. I told her my side of the business, but, really, once my front door was shut we never talked or talk boxing with each other. Albina once said : 'Whatever Henry's done he's done it himself. I've only been able to help by not nagging.' When I was away training and we talked on the telephone at nights she would never worry me with domestic things that might be going wrong. She would tell me only the things she knew would interest me and cheer me up. Four years before I actually retired she talked to me about retirement but I said that when it was time I would. She didn't then keep on about it because she knew it would unsettle me. She also has a great affection for Jim Wicks and trusts his judgment as well as my own. She came to only one of my fights—the world title fight with Muhammad Ali at Highbury Stadium, but that was only because I wanted her so much to go. I said there would never be another occasion like it, there would never be the atmosphere again, so she went. But she hated it. She was buried in the programme most of the time, and once when she did look up I'd just got my cut so she was more than ever fussed. And then she felt guilty because she reckoned she'd put the mockers on the fight, going along when she should have stayed at home! The way we went on might not have suited everyone, but it suited us. Albina would say, 'Sometimes I think the less you know the better it is.' If I had retired when she wanted me to she reckons now she would have messed everything up. Obviously we would have missed a lot of money, but those last four years meant a lot to my career in less obvious ways.

Being a boxer's wife at times can be like any businessman commuter's wife. The difference is that at the back of Albina's mind there was always the worry that, however good you were, you might get an unlucky time, and I suppose the chances of that are a little higher than sitting on the 8.15 to town. But not on the A23 or M1! A lot of people thought because I fought only three or four times a year that I must spend days lolling around the house. Well, it's true that I'm not a fellow who's got to be doing something all the time or he feels guilty. I can sit down and relax and do nothing very much quite happily. But I still had to train three times a week at the gym even when there wasn't much doing. I had Jim Wicks to meet to talk over business, which could be anything from an appearance on TV, the opening of a supermarket, or who we would like to fight next. I'd be off in the morning regularly, and back at six, or sometimes much later. Then before a fight I'd be away for five weeks without a sight of house, wife and family. That seems hard, but you have to try and learn by your mistakes, and in the first year after my marriage I learned some things the difficult way.

CHAPTER TEN

My first fight as a champion and a married man was against Roy Harris on September 13, 1960. He was carefully selected, as a world title fight with Floyd Patterson was becoming a real possibility. Harris was the Texas champion, he was in the leading ratings, and he was the first man I'd met who had fought a world heavyweight title fight—he took Patterson to the twelfth round in Los Angeles in August 1958, the referee stopping the fight. He was only the second American I had fought and I had to get into the fight gradually. He was more a boxer than a puncher, and someone had obviously told him I had a left hook, for he back-pedalled a lot and wouldn't get too close. If I hadn't carried the fight to him there wouldn't have been a fight, but I got a fairly comfortable points decision. On December 6 of that year, shortly after Henry Marco was born, we took on another guy fairly high in the ratings, the Argentinian Alex Miteff, who had fought mostly in the States in recent years and whose injury had let me in against Folley and I think, because of that victory, given me a biggish following here in Britain for the first time. Miteff was another big fellow, about 15 stone, and he'd been in the top company, but we thought he was getting slightly over the hill. I knew he had a dangerous punch so I stayed out of trouble and picked up the points with my left hand. For nine rounds the fight went well, and I was winning fairly comfortably when I got a bit careless and over-confident. In the tenth I went in and started mixing it with him, and he slung a big right-hand punch which put me down. It shook me, and I was in a bit of trouble, but my head cleared, I got up, and signalled to Jim that everything was OK. Then I got back on my old bike again, started pumping left hands, and took the decision. But it gave Jim and the Wembley crowd of 10,000 a bit of a shock.

At Wembley on March 21, 1961, I met Joe Erskine for the fourth time as a pro. In fifteen minutes the fight was over and I had won my first Lonsdale belt for my third successful defence of the British heavyweight title. At one time Joe had a thing over me. Now I had one over him. From the start I went out determined to dominate the fight from the centre of the ring. Joe had developed bad eyes, and I played on this, pumping left hands into his face all the time. He had a cut on his right eyebrow in the third round, and in the fourth the left split badly. By the fifth his eyes were bunged right up, he couldn't see and the referee couldn't do anything else but stop it.

Again, just as everything was going well, I was due for a shock, and the man responsible was Zora Folley, aided and abetted by my own errors of judgment not so much in the ring but outside it. I had beaten him three years before to break through into the top rankings. This time, however, I have to admit I didn't train properly. It wasn't so much that having beaten him once I took it easily. The trouble was, simply, that I trained at home. After this fight Jim and I sat down and came to the decision that we would never train at home again. This was a December fight, and when I got up at a quarter to four on those early winter mornings Albina might say, 'It's so cold and miserable out, give it a miss today.' It's a poor sort of boxer who blames his wife for a defeat, and I'm not trying to suggest it was anything other than my own responsibility if I turned over and went to sleep. But you sometimes have to be very strong-minded not to take the comfortable way out. I did a lot of training—Folley, after all, was still rated in the top five and he afterwards fought Cassius Clay in a world title fight—but I didn't train really hard every day. It wasn't that you were indulging in sex or anything like that. But in a home atmosphere, with a year-old baby around, you just weren't resting properly. In other ways you were too comfortable. Not that we roughed it when we were away from home, but we did our work. And another important thing : I got mean when I was away from home and family. Jim or my trainer would know about that, and they would prod me on one or two little things to see me snap and lose my temper. Then they knew I was coming to my peak. I'm a very easy-going guy normally, but after four or five weeks of training Jim didn't have to say much, just be a little bit argumentative perhaps, and I'd bite his head off. For instance he might say, 'I've told you that four times.' And I'd snap back, 'What d'you mean? You've only said it once.' Just little things, but they proved I was getting edgy and mean, and that's what you go away for. When I was at home, or not in training, such things would pass right over my head.

There was another serious problem over the Folley fight. A world title fight with Patterson was near enough on the books, and when my left shoulder began to hurt me in training I tried not to make too much of it because I knew how much this fight counted. Jim had had preliminary talks with Cus d'Amato, Patterson's manager, and we wanted a really good test before we took it. Jim and Danny could see in the gym that something was a little bit wrong, and they sent me to Bill Tucker, who specialises in the treatment of sportsmen's injuries. Bill warned me then that the wear in my left arm would stop me boxing long before eye troubles. But this was more than arthritic pain, and arthritis comes and goes. I knew we were paying out a lot of money for sparring partners, and postponements are expensive. Jim, I knew, wouldn't hesitate to pull me out of a fight no matter what the expense, so I tried to put the twinges out of my mind. I thought to myself, 'I may not be 100 per cent but I'll get by.'

Of course I didn't get by. Folley gave me one of the three major lickings of my boxing life, though in my own defence it was no disgrace to be beaten by a fighter of his quality. Folley was a box-puncher, who could box your ears off and knock them off as well. At once I knew my distance was out; I couldn't find the range with my left hand. On the notes I made at the time I said, 'Boxed very bad and distance very bad.' In the second round I came right on to a short right hand to the chin. Folley had a really good right hand, and I was down and truly out. But all the same it was a lesson which needed to be learned. That was the last time Albina saw me in the five weeks before a fight. It was also the last occasion I took any chance on being all right on the night. The more experienced you get the more you realise it doesn't work like that. That was one of the worst mistakes of my career. No one feels sorry for you when the fight is over, and it's no good making excuses. The irony so far as Patterson was concerned was that instead of taking me he took Liston. And Liston knocked him out in the first round, wallop! Patterson never got his title back. That was the second time I just missed a world title fight. After Johansson stopped Patterson for the title in the third round in June 1959 we started negotiations to meet the Swede. But the following June Patterson won back the title by knocking out Johansson in the fifth and so we lost our chance there.

Usually there was so much concentration on my eyes by the press that other sorts of injury or ailment, like the arthritis or the wear in my elbow, slipped by with only those on the inside knowing. As I mentioned earlier, in my first pro fight with Joe Erskine, I banged my hand on his hard nut with my left hand and it came up so big that at the finish of the fight it was like a balloon. They had to cut the glove off to release my hand. But the first damage to the knuckle was done not in this fight but in an amateur bout with Erskine several years before. The knuckle was split and swollen, but in the Army you didn't have quite the medical care you would have as a professional boxer, and they just told me to rest it. I did for a while, then carried on boxing. After the 1955 Erskine fight I went to Bill Tucker, who said he could treat it. The knuckle was as big as a golf ball, and he explained that eventually the stuff under the swelling would calcify and go hard. Then I would have problems in opening and closing my hand. He said if he operated at once and took the stuff away it would look just like chewing gum. But rather than operate he preferred to disperse it with injections, massage and hot wax. 'You'll have to come here every day for eight weeks if we do that,' he told me. So that's what I did, every day, Sundays excepted, and by the time he finished the knuckle was like a pin cushion. It had had more needles in it than a porcupine's back. The hand had to be bandaged to make sure there was no infection, but I had no more serious trouble with it. Actually, it was a bit of an asset, because there was always a bit of a lump there even after I'd taped my hands before a fight. When we went abroad they always fiddled and poked, thinking I had something under the bandage, but it was just knuckle with this slight permanent swelling. You can see it today and I still can't quite straighten the finger.

But going back to Folley, I needed another fight quickly to get my confidence back, and on January 23, 1962, we took Tony Hughes, the American protégé of Rocky Marciano. He was from Texas, and not the toughest guy in the world, strangely enough. Also, with Rocky coming, we knew there would be plenty of publicity attached to it. I had only seen Marciano on film, although our careers overlapped to the extent that he first won the world title in 1952, and held it until he retired undefeated in 1955, a year after George and me turned pro. If ever boxing produced a Jekyll and Hyde it was Marciano. Outside the ring he was the quietest, most softly spoken guy you could wish to meet. If you were in a crowd of people he would be in a corner hardly saying a word. And yet when he was in the ring it was organised murder; it was war. People close to him in America have told me stories about him. One said to him once, 'You took a bit of a liberty there, Rocky. You hit Cockell when he was on the floor.' He was talking about one of Marciano's seven title fights when he stopped Don Cockell, the British heavyweight champion of the time, in May 1955, in the ninth round. Rocky wouldn't believe him. They had to show him photographs and film of him hitting the man, because he never knew himself he was doing it. If he missed with a punch he would follow through with an elbow. If a man was going down, on his knees, he'd carry on punching him. But at the Anglo-American Sporting Club, where I met him, that was almost impossible to believe. They reckon, too, Marciano was one of only two fighters in America who would have mothers in their scores bringing their babies to him to have him kiss them. The other was Joe Louis. It was a tragedy when Marciano was killed in an air crash in the prime of his life. He was one man I would never like to have met in the ring. His protégé, Tony Hughes, fortunately, was a good deal less formidable and I stopped him with a left hook in the fifth.

The next build-up fight was against Wayne Bethea, a big, coloured American, at Belle Vue, Manchester. He'd been around a few years and was a useful heavyweight, a bit over the top. He knew the game, though, and was belting them around a bit on the Continent, like Dick Richardson. I came in at 13 stone 7 and won fairly well on points. It was about this time that we decided that 13–7 to 8 was my best weight and we rarely went in at anything else after that. On April 2, 1962, I went in against Joe Erskine, for the seventh and last time, for my British and Empire titles. Joe was now past his best. He was getting puffy round the eyes, and I worked on that. The left hand was going well and soon he had swellings and cuts on both eyes. One eye was completely closed; he had a cut on it and God knows what. It was a pretty bloody fight. The referee stopped it in the ninth round, and that was Joe's last big fight.

On March 26, 1963, at Wembley Pool I fought Dick Richardson for the second time. This was a fight where we had a little go at each other after the bell. He slung a punch at the end of the third and I came back at him; you just had to with a fighter like Dick. He and Brian London were real boxing 'bully boys'. If you let them get on top they would bash the life out of you. If they slung a punch after the bell you had no alternative but to come back otherwise they would have got a real psychological boost. My policy was never to let them get away with anything. That's the way it was with the third round incident—and it knocked the wind out of Dick a bit, too! Some said Dick was mad because I hit him after the ref had shouted 'Break'. But if you come out of a clinch and the ref hasn't said anything then you are entitled to hit. That's what I did and that's where Dick got mixed up. I'm not trying to make myself out to be an angel. Now and again I let a punch slip on the break. But on this particular occasion I wasn't guilty. Dick would always come out fishing with his head. On this occasion he caught me in the first round and I had a cut eye. But the left hook was going well and in the fifth round I landed with three so that he was back against the ropes, and another to the jaw put him down. That was all the top British opposition for the time being. Now the wires began to hum over a fight with another top American—Cassius Clay.

Mum and Dad

Bern, George (middle)
and me

I'm the twin on the left

The British Olympic boxing team, Helsinki 1952. From left to right: Tom Parkinson, Eddie Hearn, Alf Galley, Percy Lewis, Terry Gooding, Tommy Nicholls, Johnny Maloney, Dai Dower, Peter Waterman, Freddie Reardon, Henry Cooper, Bernie Forster, Harry Mallin, Jas Macintosh

L/Cpl Henry Cooper, 'Boxers' Battalion', RAOC

Sparring with Alonzo Johnson

Roadwork (me on the left)

Skipping

TRAINING

Heavy bag

Speed ball

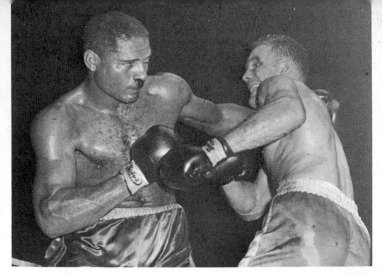

My first fight – and a win – against a world class American heavyweight, Zora Folley, at Wembley on October 14, 1958. I've slipped
inside his left lead, ready to sling a left hook at his exposed jaw

This really scared us. In the fifth – and last – round of Joe Erskine's
challenge for my British and Empire titles at Earls Court on
November 17, 1961, I put him down. We thought Joe had broken
his back on the ropes

Cassius Clay gets the old left hook in the fourth round of our first fight, at Wembley Stadium on July 19, 1963. Tommy Smith, the referee, moves in to start the count

This blow-up of a Cassius Clay left jab clearly shows the split in the glove that finished off my damaged eye in the fifth round

This is Your Life at Thames TV, with (from left to right) Harry Painter, Bob Hill, Jim Wicks, Albina and behind her Billy Walker, Jack Bodell behind me and Dick Richardson behind Dad, George, Bern and Eamonn Andrews

If a picture tells a story, this one tells what Jim, George and I thought of Harry Gibbs's verdict in my last fight, against Joe Bugner in defence of my British and Commonwealth titles at Wembley on March 16, 1971

At home, with Henry Marco, Albina, John Pietro, and some of the trophies I've collected over the years

CHAPTER ELEVEN

When Cassius Clay came to England to fight me at Wembley Football Stadium on June 18, 1963, some of the press here tended to write him down. He had beaten only six men who could have been rated as anything more than second-class heavyweights, they said, and there was only one world famous name among them—Archie Moore, who at the time was forty-nine, old enough to be Clay's father. At twenty-one Clay was supposed to be pretty raw. We knew about him from Fleischer's annual, from all we'd read about him and of course from Bill Daly and our other contacts in the USA. He'd won the Olympic light-heavyweight title in Rome, in 1960, and since turning pro he'd shot up to be No. 2 contender to the champion, Sonny Liston—Patterson was still No. 1. We knew he was a flashy type of fighter with an enormous reach, and we'd heard about his ranting and his raving and his prediction lark. But raw? To my mind he'd beaten some useful boys on the way up, and in the next fight after me he won the world title.

Directly he got here he was up to his games. It was Cooper for the chop in round five. And he would hold up his hand with the fingers and thumb spread out just to make sure the photographers got the message. Friends kept asking me, 'Are you worried by all that talk?' I'd been too long a professional. 'No, let him carry on,' I'd say. 'I'm on the gate. He's selling tickets and earning me good money.' That wasn't strictly accurate. I was on a fixed fee and it didn't matter if two people or 200,000 turned up. But we did have a percentage of ancillary rights—TV, cinema and so on—and the more people became interested the more we were going to get out of it. Clay knew exactly what he was about. It was all a gimmick, and he'd copied it from an American wrestler called Gorgeous George, who had a mop of blond curly hair, and when he went into the ring a big velvet train with two girls to hold it. They would perfume his corner, and then he'd go round the ring shouting, 'I am the prettiest. I am the greatest.' Clay thought that would be a good gimmick for him. And that explained his antics·when he came over in 1963.

Although it was only a ten-round fight it meant a lot to

my world standing. We trained for this at the Fellowship Inn, a big pub on the Bellingham estate run by good friends of ours, Les and Ann Denny. They had a big ballroom at the back of the pub, and we transformed this into a gymnasium. We'd decided I should be away from home for five weeks this time, and that it would be a gradual build-up to the fight. Mum and Dad had recently left Bellingham and were living at Hounslow where I'd bought them a cigarette, confectionery and packet grocery business. So although we were on familiar grounds at Bellingham there were no other distractions. We lived in rooms at the front of the pub, away from any noise, and I suppose about a hundred to a hundred and fifty people would come most days to watch us in training, a good many of them familiar faces. Someone would take a box round and we'd get quite a useful sum for the old age pensioners or some other charity. It was quite an event in Bellingham.

We'd especially shipped over an American Negro boxer called Alonzo Johnson as sparring partner. Alonzo had an interesting background. He'd fought Clay in Clay's home town of Louisville, and they'd judged him to lose narrowly on points. Alonzo always reckoned he'd beaten Clay, and even Cassius admits he was given a hell of a fight. In fact he was still using Johnson as a sparring partner on his visit to Britain and Europe in 1971. But the thing about Alonzo was that he could imitate Clay's style beautifully. At Bellingham he boarded at a house just down the road from us, but he ate at the pub with us and did quite well out of it. We paid him five hundred dollars, his fare and his keep, and on the night he was very much for us. He reckoned he'd had a rough deal in his fight with Clay and was hoping I could get a bit of revenge for him.

I met Clay for the first time on the BBC's *Sportsview* programme a few days before the fight. I shook hands but that was enough. You are never all that friendly at an official reception beforehand because you know you've got to be doing your work next day, and the object of that work is to belt the other guy to defeat as soon as you possibly can. I was glad that Clay stayed on one side of the room and me on the other. I never liked to get too friendly before a fight; afterwards was different.

At the weigh-in Clay was better than I expected. He

hadn't got to that stage where he seemed to go potty. There was one later occasion, against Sonny Liston, when the doctor was in two minds whether to let him fight because of his blood pressure. Another time they were threatening to fine him if he said another word. He was still talking plenty, gesturing with his hand that I would go in five rounds. He'd had one or two predictions came off at that point, but that was only by good luck rather than judgment. The best fighter in the world cannot say he is going to do things a certain way and be sure it will happen. Naturally he was trying to beat me in the fifth round, but it takes two to make a fight, and what your opponent does or how he will react can often defy reason.

We had a strategy worked out. We knew he was going to be fast, but it's not until you are in there with him that you realise just how fast he really is. In the first round my problem was to try and get in distance to land my punches. It's not that Clay is ever going to hurt you—he doesn't, really —but he is such a tall man that he can always outreach you. He was a stone and a half heavier than me at that time, and he must have had the longest reach in the game—between four and five inches longer than me. From finger tip to finger tip he was seventy-nine inches. You feel a man out in the first round, and jabbing away I found I was six inches short. I am thinking, 'I'm in distance here,' but I'm not. And bump! —Clay's scoring. His reflexes were so good. He did all sorts of unorthodox things. He would jerk his head backwards out of the way of punches, which as a kid you were taught you should never do. You were supposed to slip inside and try to counter-punch. He wouldn't worry about that. He was on the move continuously, and as far as I am concerned he is—or was—the fastest heavyweight of all time. There was never a still target in front of you. Directly the ropes touch his back he was away. Our campaign was to back him on to the ropes or into a corner because the only way you could stop him moving was to trap him there. I would jab once, then I'd double jab. He'd jerk his head back to the first, then the second, and I'd sling in yet another jab, and he'd jerk back from that too. He could judge a punch to the last quarter inch. What with his height and his reach and his reflexes he had a lot of advantages. He couldn't counter-punch with a great deal of power, not as he might if he were slipping inside punches. But after his jerks he could still come back with a sneaky right hand. In general he was a damaging rather than a knock-out puncher. He was a flicker with his left hand and a long puncher. You never saw him sling a punch that only travelled six inches. It was always a long-arm punch, and that type was always more likely to drag and tear your skin than the short sharp punches of the really hard hitters. That, anyway, was my estimation of him in the first round, which was pretty even. I was doing all the forcing and Clay all the dancing around. I might just have shaved it I suppose.

In the second round I knew I had to pressure him a bit more and trap him on the ropes. I had to be prepared to take a bit more punishment. When you're being outreached by three or four inches you can't stand off and try to box a man. Part of my plan was to keep a moving target in front of him. I was bobbing and weaving more than I reckoned to normally. Clay was a bomp! bomp! man. His corner would be shouting, 'Stick and move, stick and move,' stick being the American term for jab. If I had stood still I would have been picked off easily. I was also trying to crouch a little more with my head down and my hands held high. In the second round I could see where Clay was still amateurish. He was a novice at in-fighting; he really had no idea at all. When I caught him off the ropes and he came into a clinch he just held me and waited until the referee said break. I tried to be as rough as I could inside. I really roughed him up. I belted him to the body, tried to upper-cut him on the inside, pushed him, anything almost except using the elbows. I often say that while you are doing something dirty you could be doing something clean! He didn't like it at all, and kept on looking at the referee. All the time he just scraped out of trouble though. One or two of my punches missed by a quarter of an inch, no more. But you've got to give Clay credit. He could play to margins as narrow as that.

We were pleased with the way it was going. Jim said, 'Just keep that up.' But in the third round I hit trouble, with my eye starting to bleed. At the time I thought it was a clash of heads, but looking at the film afterwards I could see differently. Towards the end of the round he threw a long, loopy left hook, and then was going to follow it with a right. I came at him and he shortened the punch, chopping down with his right on my left eye and slitting it badly. Jim wanted to stop the fight there and then. But I argued with him in the corner between rounds three and four. After all the training you don't want to give up too easily, and by the time we'd finished arguing the timekeeper said, 'Seconds out.' I was now sure I could reach him. I'd done so in the third a few times, and I knew I could get at him inside. My cut was a very bad one. The cuts I had in my two fights with Clay were the worst of my career. This one was one and a half to two inches long. Danny worked like hell on it. He had the treatment off to a fine art. The Americans talk of their expert cut men, but Danny was as good as any of them, and with his adrenalin-vaseline compound he stopped the bleeding. All the same, in the fourth I knew the eye was bad and it was now or never. At times I left myself exposed but that was the chance I had to take. I went after Clay, throwing as many left hooks as I could, hoping that one would land. Suddenly I had him. I jabbed once, twice, three times. Each time he went back, back, back. But now he was right back on the ropes and he couldn't go any farther. The fourth punch hit him, a genuine left hook, a more curved punch compared with the jab, out to in, and all my power behind it. The ropes helped make that situation, but they also saved Clay. If I'd caught him in the centre of the ring there would have been nothing to break his fall, and it's the fall on to the canvas where you hit your head that shakes you up as much as the punch. If he had fallen more heavily I don't think he would have got up. As it was he slid gently down the ropes, there was a count of five, Clay started to get up and then the bell went. For Clay to get up like that was really a classic boxing error which he was lucky to get away with. It's the mistake a guy can make who has never been on the floor before. When you are down you should stay down for as long as possible. Your head may clear, but you have to consider your legs as well, and the longer you rest the more the strength will come back into them. It's what the old-timers mean by taking the long count. Clay wanted to prove he hadn't been hurt, but he walked back to his corner like a drunk.

You can see from the film how they worked on him in the corner. Oh boy! If it had all happened in the second minute of the second round I think there would have been a very different verdict. Clay would have jumped up at five exactly the same as he did, and at that time, once I had an opponent groggy, I finished them off. I was in my prime at twenty-nine—heavyweights mature late—and there's no doubt in my mind that if he had got up like that with his arms hanging down by his sides he wouldn't have got off the hook. He was an open target—and he was big enough to hit!

Anyway, in Clay's corner there was a right old panic during the interval. Angelo Dundee, his trainer, and one or two of the millionaire syndicate backing him were up there and then came the next big incident. Suddenly they found Clay had a split glove. All the press were round the ringside, and none of them had seen a split glove during the boxing, but by the time the referee had been called over to the corner, seen one of the stewards, the steward had gone to the back of the hall to try to find a spare set of gloves, discovered there weren't any, and gone back to tell the corner, easily half to three-quarters of a minute must have gone by. Now half a minute to a fit man is a lifetime. When you're really trained up you need only twenty seconds and you are back to your old self.

Jim was going to stop the fight at the end of the third, but after all this he had to let me come out again for the fifth round just in case Clay was still a little groggy. While they hunted round for replacement gloves the referee, Tommy Smith, possibly thought he was doing me a favour in getting the fight going again after a full minute and three-quarters. Against that, Clay's right glove was split with a big hunk of stuffing gone. If he'd wrapped glasspaper round his fist he couldn't have done better against an eye like mine. With the second or third punch of that round he caught me bang on the eye, which started to gush again. You don't actually *feel* a bad cut. It just stings and goes numb. What tells you it's a bad one is when you feel the warm blood dripping on your body, and, boy! I could feel it this time just like a tap pouring on to my chest. I thought, this is bad, and then Clay started to come forward, for the only time, slinging punches as hard as he could. I've heard him say that blood sickens him, that he could hear me bleeding, that he couldn't bring himself to hit me, and so on. Well, he may have had those humanitarian thoughts afterwards. All I know is that at the time, in the ring, directly he

saw his advantage he came right in after me, just as I would
have done against him. The only times he ever came forward, both in 1963 and in the world title fight three years
later, I had blood pouring from the eye and couldn't see.
Jim shouted 'Stop it, ref!' and was up on the apron of the
ring before the referee had actually done so. It was that bad.
I've got quick healing skin, as I've said, but though a cut
heals on the surface it takes time to knit together and get
strong again underneath. That one took several months and
partly for that reason my next fight was not until the following February, against Brian London at Manchester for the
British, Empire and European championships.

CHAPTER TWELVE

Between the first Clay fight in June 1963 and the second for
the world title, in May 1966, I had eight fights, six of which
I won and two I lost. I won the European championship
and then was robbed of it outside the ring. I took my second
Lonsdale belt for successfully defending the British championship six times, and had my quickest ever win. But life
always had its downs to go with the ups. I went in with a
greengrocer's business and suffered more worries and loss of
sleep through it than I did before any fight, and that in-
cludes the world championship.

At Belle Vue, Manchester, on February 24, 1964, I was
meeting Brian London for the third time. I'd knocked him
out in the first round in May 1956 and won the British
championship for the first time when I beat him on points in
January 1959. That fight was one of the hardest I ever had.
This one was comparatively easy. Although it went fifteen
rounds I was on top most of the time and, a big relief, I
suffered no cuts, which after the Clay fight was quite something. Apart from taking my second Lonsdale belt, the
fight was chiefly memorable for the scrap which went on
outside the ring with the Boxing Board of Control. This
was the first fight we boxed under a new rule covering the
tape that goes round your hands. The Board suddenly announced that they were allowing only three yards of tape. At
a title fight the Board steward in charge brings your tape

and bandages into your dressing-room, you tape your hands in front of him, and he stamps them.

The night the steward brought in the tape as usual. Danny Holland starts to cut it and says, 'There's not a lot here for his hand.' The steward answers, 'That's not for one hand, that's for two.' Jim can't believe it. 'Both his hands?' he asks. 'That's right,' says the steward. 'You'd better get Onslow Fane,' says Jim, in that kind of voice. Mr Fane, the President of the Board, sends word that he's not in charge that evening. So Jim asks for Teddy Waltham, Secretary of the Board. But Teddy isn't having any. 'I'm not in charge,' he sends back. 'Right,' says Jim, 'fetch Harry Levene.' Harry is the promoter, and George, my brother, goes to get him. The ten green bottles had nothing on this! 'What time are we on the radio?' George asks Harry. 'At 9.30,' Harry answers. 'Well, at 9.30 we'll still be sitting in this dressing-room unless you get Fane and Waltham to sort this out.' Now, Harry's a business man, he'd signed contracts with the BBC and he knew what had to be done. He brought the officials into our dressing-room, and it was graciously admitted that there had been a mistake, that the bandage was not for two hands but one, and Mr Fane measured out another three yards for the second hand. But it was still too little, and when I came out of the ring my left hand was heavily swollen where I had knocked it on London's head. There's no doubt that the lack of adequate bandaging was the cause of the damage. Too much tape and bandage can be a hindrance, but when you land a blow your fingers literally spread with the pressure of it. You need adequate bandage to help contain it.

Apart from this incident, I was pleased by the London fight. Brian had slimmed down a bit at that time, and he'd been having a bit of success on the Continent. I wanted to stay out of trouble and not get cut, and concentrate on the boxing. It all went as I hoped, and it was a pleasant feeling to have made a bit of history by being the first heavyweight to win a second Lonsdale belt for close on fifty years, and also to be the European champion—the title had become vacant through the retirement of Ingemar Johanssen. Quickly, though, I found that a European title could sometimes be more bother than it is worth. I pay a manager twenty-five per cent to manage me. When you win a European championship you don't need a manager. They say, 'You've got to defend your title against so-and-so from Germany or Italy.' And if no promoter puts in for that fight, then it goes to purse offers. It happens a lot on the Continent because that way the promoter gets the fight cheaper. He can get the fight for about £8,000 with sixty per cent for the champion and forty per cent for the challenger. But £4,000 to £5,000 was no good to us. Jim was there to do his best for me, and we were getting about £20,000 a fight at that time, less tax. We didn't want to be managed by the European Boxing Union on their terms.

Quickly, too, we ran up against problems in getting European fights here in Britain. At that time the chief contenders for the European title were Germans, and nearly all the promoters in this country were Jewish. You simply wouldn't get a Jew promoting a fight involving a German. With none of our promoters bidding, the German promoters could make their offers really cheap. Jim was saying at the time, 'I won't let him take his coat off for under ten grand,' and he meant it. In the end we agreed to take on Karl Mildenberger, the German champion, in Germany, but trouble was on the way. After two weeks' training I felt the old pains in the left elbow, and Pip Newman and Bill Tucker, the two top specialists in London, both examined me and said that two weeks' rest was necessary. So we got the German promoter and an EBU representative over, and even took them to the specialists to show them X-rays. So they said all right, we will put the fight back a fortnight. I said, 'What good is that to me? I've got to rest it completely for a fortnight. I won't be properly trained.' The promoter claimed he could only get the hall on limited occasions, and that there was no other date possible. I said, 'We shan't be ready if that's the case,' and that was how it was left. The next we heard was that the EBU had stripped me of the title, Mildenberger went on to win it, and that helped put him in line for a world championship fight with Clay. We were pretty fed up with the German boxing people—it wasn't so long before that they had withheld that £700 after the fight with Schoeppner. Later, Mildenberger was injured when he was due to defend his European championship and the EBU postponed the fight for a month! It was a blatant example of how unfairly the EBU rules sometimes worked.

On November 16, 1964, I took on Richard Rischer, an American, and promptly hit trouble. If anyone asks me which fight of my career I want to remember least, then this is about it. It was my worst fight since I lost four in succession in 1956–7. Rischer was a real spoiler. He was pretty experienced, and it was only afterwards we found that none of the top American boys ever wanted to fight him. They just couldn't look good against him, and I quickly found out why. He held you, he messed you around, he pulled you, he hugged, he cuffed, he did everything except let you show you could box. It was a combination of things, I suppose, because when I had an off night it was really off, and this was a right stinkeroo. I couldn't get working, I couldn't get any rhythm. A boxer likes everything to flow in the ring, but that night it wouldn't. I'd rather have fought a giant spider. Anyway, I lost the verdict on points over ten rounds and, as far as the next fights were concerned, put it out of my mind. It wasn't that important a fight really, and I had some good wins to come afterwards. But it was one of our mistakes, one of our few mis-matches. All boxers get them, some worse than others. I remember Bruce Woodcock, a really good British champion in my opinion, taking on two US fighters, Tami Mauriello and Joe Baksi, who did him no good at all. When he went to America to fight for the first time he met Mauriello, who was a hell of a tough fighter and had given their top men a lot of trouble. It was silly to take on that calibre of fighter so early in his career. Bruce was a good boxer and a good puncher; he had a great right hand. But when he fought Baksi he got his jaw smashed so badly that splinters of bone travelled up and affected one of his eyes. He was in a pitch dark room for several weeks because of the danger to his sight. Baksi was a really dangerous fighter. If he had had the right mental approach, if he had taken the game more seriously, he could have been a world champion. But there was a bit of the playboy about him and he hated training. At that time there was a clutch of good American fighters, Rocky Marciano, Ezzard Charles, Jersey Joe Walcott, Archie Moore, Joey Maxim, Lee Oma, Gus Lesnevich and so on. I wouldn't have minded being around at that time, because I think I could have held my own with a few of them. I don't say beaten them necessarily, but it would have been interesting. I'm only glad I wasn't around for Marciano—I'm quite happy he'd finished.

In the eight fights between the two Clay matches, six of my opponents were Americans. Next on the list was Dick Wipperman at the Royal Albert Hall on January 12, 1965. He was a big, tall man, and yet another cowboy, so we were told (somehow I missed out on the Indians). He was a left-hand merchant, like myself, and for the first two rounds he was matching me with the jab. I was getting plenty in the face and so was he. But then I got in the hook and that was it. He wilted away to such an extent that the referee stopped the fight in the fifth. I can't think of one fight which I finished with a right to the body. The finishing punch was always the same, the good old left hook.

The next fight, against Chip Johnson, another American, gave me a lot of satisfaction. It was at the Civic Hall, Wolverhampton, one of my luckiest arenas, on April 20, 1965. Only five months earlier Johnson had effectively finished George's career at the Free Trade Hall, Manchester. George had boxed badly, and the fight was stopped in the third round with George suffering a badly cut eye. George wasn't getting the fights, and what with everything he decided it was time to call it a day. I was pleased to get this fellow now. He was one of those who talked a lot. 'What I've done to one I can do to the other,' and all that sort of thing. 'I'll be up there in the world ratings after this,' he was saying in his press build up. I thought, 'Oh, yeah, you'll just suit me. . . .' The revenge angle was being played up pretty big, and as far as I was concerned quite legitimately. It was one I wanted to win above most. And as it turned out I didn't have to wait long. Suddenly he gave me an opening in the first round, and I was too old to miss gifts. Wallop! It was a good left hook, and his old legs had the quivers as he went down. He was well out. It was one of my quickest knock-outs and gave me a taste for the Civic at Wolverhampton. Later there I stopped Jefferson Davis in one round and Jack Bodell in the second. Three pay days inside four rounds gives you a genuine feeling for a place.

My next fight was also in the Midlands, against Johnny Prescott for the British and Empire title on June 17, 1965. The fight was in the open air at St Andrews, the Birmingham City football ground, and it had to be postponed for two days because of rain. It was the first time I'd met Prescott, though I knew he was making a name for himself as a glamour boy. Both he and Jack Bodell at that time were under the same manager, George Biddles. Prescott was stealing most of the limelight from Jack, and for the first eight rounds he put up a pretty fair show. But in the tenth round he was tired from the punishment he took to the body, and I put him down for counts of two and eight. At the end of the round Biddles retired him, which was just as well, for the rain started coming down again.

About this time Jim started his negotiations for a world title fight with Clay, who was in process of re-naming himself Muhammad Ali. I'd had good wins over Chip Johnson and Wipperman, and we knew if I could keep up in the world ratings then it could well be on. So I choose this moment to get beaten! The fighter responsible was a coloured American boy called Amos Johnson—no relation to Chip—who was approaching the top ratings. I think I was a trifle unlucky. In my notes at the time I said, 'Boxed badly but thought I just won.' This was an all-heavyweight bill at Wembley Pool with Johnny Prescott, Billy Walker and Jack Bodell all fighting. It was the champion, Henry Cooper, who had to go and stink the place out!

Like Roger Rischer, Johnson was a spoiler, and the referee let him get away with almost everything. I was hit low on two occasions, certainly low enough for him to be disqualified, and that took me right out of my stride. Both punches were in the groin, which is weakening and hurtful, and that, in combination with my own bad form, made it a real off-nght. All the same, I think I was unlucky not to get the verdict.

Disappointing as it was, an event occurred in December, 1965, which more than compensated and, according to Jim Wicks, made a big difference in my life. One day towards the end of the year a gilt-edged card dropped through my letter box saying simply, 'Her Majesty the Queen and H.R.H. Prince Philip, Duke of Edinburgh, invite Mr Henry Cooper to lunch at Buckingham Palace.'

CHAPTER THIRTEEN

The Queen's invitation card to lunch was not a total surprise. Things are more organised at the Palace than that. Several days before the card arrived, Jim Wicks had a phone call. Right out of the blue this chap says would Mr Henry Cooper like to lunch with the Royal Family. Jim nearly told him to get off the phone and stop larking about. But he checked himself, and said well, of course I would, anyone would. 'OK then,' said the fellow. Jim still thought it might be one of our friends pulling our legs, because so many of them make jokes of that sort. But this voice sounded genuine enough for Jim to hold himself back. 'But don't go building your hopes up,' Jim warned me. When the card dropped through the letter box we were much relieved, and so was Jim that he hadn't let rip. Albina was so nervous and excited she didn't know what to do first, run out and tell all the neighbours or send my best suit to the cleaners. I had been to the Palace once before, to a cocktail party as a member of the 1952 Olympic team. But this was a private luncheon party with half a dozen of us sitting down with the Royal Family, which was something fantastic. They hold these informal lunches about twice a year, and we were very lucky because the Royal children, Princess Anne and Prince Charles, were at home as well.

The dress was ordinary lounge suit, so Albina made sure the old creases were razor sharp. 'Have you got your invitation card?' If she said it once she said it a hundred times. She was sure they wouldn't let me in without it. Jim Wicks and the family rang me to wish me well—it was worse than a big-fight night. I had an Alfa-Romeo at the time and they said we could come in our own car and park it at the Palace. No chance of a ticket there, I thought. I pulled up at Buckingham Palace gates, and the old rozzer took a quick look at the invitation, gave me a smile and said, 'All right, Henry, straight through.' Some press photographers were waiting at the gates, most of them old pals, and they wanted to know if I'd come back after I had parked the car and get a few shots of me inside the Palace yard. So I found a spot for the

Alfa and walked back towards the gates. I couldn't keep a smile off my face as I thought of the times as a kid I'd peered through the railings watching the Guards. And here I was in that self-same place going to lunch with the Queen!

Inside the Palace the Queen's equerry, Lord Plunket, met me and showed me into the ante-room, where I was introduced to the other guests. Among them I remembered Nigel Patrick, the actor, Sir Christopher Cockerell who invented the hovercraft, Alison Westwood the show jumper, and Alan Bullock the historian. We had all been around, but we were a bit on edge, and as they served cocktails Lord Plunket tried to put us at our ease. I didn't drink much so I had an orange juice, which gave me something to do with my hands. Then it was explained that we would line up so that as the Royal Family came in we could be introduced. Then the Queen and the other members of the family would talk to us individually until we were called for lunch. We could all sit down once the Queen herself was seated. It sounded a little formal, and we at once lined up when we heard the words, 'The Queen is coming.' Then the most marvellous thing happened to relax everyone. The doors opened and two or three Corgis came pattering in. We all bent down to pat them and that broke the ice. A few moments later the Royal Family came in, but somehow it was funny to see these dogs running round in such palatial surroundings with all that priceless furniture. The Queen talked to several of us for about five or ten minutes, and she knew just what to say. She must do a lot of homework. She knew what was going on in the boxing world at that time and she knew exactly what to say to me. There had been some conjecture in the papers about a world title fight with Clay, and Prince Philip asked me what I thought the chances were of it taking place (in fact it was five months later). We also chatted about the Olympics and equestrian events.

In the dining room I was fortunate enough to sit next to Princess Anne, who was fifteen at the time. It was amazing what an easy girl she was to talk to, and how she, too, had learned to put people at their ease. There were one or two little things that I noticed. When the wine waiter came round I had some but the Princess had a Cola. I said, 'Do you drink?' and laughed. 'Oh, no,' she said. 'Well—I do when Mummy's not there. At school Mummy came once and she saw us drinking a cocktail and she told me off. Mummy and Daddy don't like me drinking, so while I'm here I only have soft drinks.' She was just like any other girl talking about her Mum. We got on to sport and dogs, and I said, 'Corgis are your trade mark aren't they.' She said, 'No, I prefer a big dog. I've got a Labrador of my own but Mummy prefers Corgis.' It was so nice because most of the ordinary people in the street put the Royal Family on a pedestal—well, I do, I'm a royalist—and here was Princess Anne talking about Mummy and Daddy and all her likes and dislikes just like any other girl.

The table was immaculate—it was a large oval of dark polished wood with beautiful cutlery and china. There was no table-cloth, just mats. It was a fairly intimate dining-room, not a great big hall. It was how you would imagine the Queen's dining-room would be for entertaining small numbers of guests. The flunkeys who waited on you were all done up in white gloves and wigs and breeches. Afterwards we moved into another room for coffee and liqueurs for those who wanted them, and Prince Charles came over for a chat. He was at Gordonstoun then and I asked him if he boxed there. He said no, but it was a pretty tough, spartan sort of life all the same. Cold showers and up at seven for a run whatever the weather. It reminded me of my training. Then the Queen came up again for another talk—she made a point of speaking afterwards with anyone she had not spoken to before lunch. Then she and the family left. I was struck by what a beautiful woman she is, more so than she appears in photographs, and she doesn't wear a lot of make-up. When you see film stars at the cinema they look lovely, but when you meet them you can often see all kinds of spots and blemishes. The Queen's skin and colouring are jolly nearly flawless, and she was wearing a very pretty green dress which made her look lovely. She's so much more petite than she looks in photos. Philip is one of the boys—one of the chaps—someone you can take to immediately. He loves a joke, you feel he'll look at a pretty girl and appreciate her, he's simply a man's man.

This was one of the really important moments of my life. Let's face it, life is an education, and the older you get the more you should learn, and the more things rub off on you. It's at times like these that you feel proud and honoured, and think you are getting somewhere. I'm a royalist, like I've said, so I was especially proud. I like the idea of a hereditary Royal Family better than a presidential system. After all, they aren't governing the country, they are figureheads, and I prefer people like them to a president who could be a con man, and there have been plenty of presidents recently who have been con men. We've had a king or queen for centuries—it's our tradition, it's unique, and I think we should stick to it. I can't understand people who are anti-royal. The chances of a bad king or queen ruining the country are pretty remote these days. But you can have a bad president who can lead a country into God knows what and get away with it.

After all that excitement it was back to business with a fight against another American, Hubert Hilton, at Olympia, London. The only trouble with Olympia was the smell. It was used for a circus as well, and there was always this terrible smell of animals hanging round the place. The ring was, in fact, in the sawdust circus ring. The dressing-rooms were on the floor above, and you had to walk down the staircase and across a fair bit of forecourt to get to the arena. Hilton was another coloured, rather flashy type of boxer, ranked No 9 in the world. I dumped a left hook on him after one minute fifteen seconds of the second round and the referee stopped the fight. 'Boxed well, felt good,' I noted at the time. My weight had varied here a bit. I was 13 stone 10½ for that fight, where two fights before I was 13 stone 4½. Then, on February 16 at Wolverhampton, came another good win, a 100 second knock-out of Jefferson Davis, another boxer from the American South, from Mobile, Alabama. He even wore a stetson to try and prove something about his cowboy history. He had gone ten rounds with Ernie Terrell, and he had stopped my brother George in seven rounds with a cut eye in October 1963. So it was all good publicity when I clobbered him with the fastest knock-out of my career.

CHAPTER FOURTEEN

At that point I was maturing with age. The little guys tend to burn themselves out. I was nice and relaxed inside and outside the ring, I was in the world's top five and it was all going well. About this time the prospect of another fight with Clay, this time for his world title, was looming up. Lots of people claim they had a hand in the deal, and one way or another quite a few did. Clay was due for military service at this time and was about to have his medical and go before the draft board in Louisville, Kentucky. If he was made 1-Y it would exempt him from military service. If it was 1-A he would be eligible. But Clay by this time had started to call himself Muhammad Ali on assuming the Muslim faith, and was swearing that he would not be called up. There was very little straight matching going on at this point. There was usually uproar behind the scenes with better fights going on outside the ring than in. Promoters, managers and matchmakers were all at it.

One day we had Michael X, the Black Power man, call us saying he would like to discuss something to our advantage. So, nothing to lose, Jim made a date to meet him at a place near Baker Street in a big private house. I think there was a Muslim holiday and hundreds of coloured fellows were milling around. They were waiting to kiss his hands and his feet, and he gives Jim the big-I-am stuff, 'I'm sorry, I can't speak now, my people need me.' And he passes Jim on to an American Negro who says they can get me a world title fight with Ali. Jim says, 'You'd better talk with Harry Levene, he's the promoter', and left. The fight was eventually signed through a quite separate set of negotiations, but they still came back asking to be reimbursed. They didn't get any change, I might add.

Meantime, George Chuvalo, the Canadian champion, had challenged me to defend my Empire title at Toronto on April 18. But as Jim always said, he was 'too ugly'. We only liked good-looking fighters! Anyway, that was as good an excuse as any. Chuvalo was a rough handful, but the silly thing really was the money they offered. Canada was always way behind Britain or the United States for money. They offered 25,000 Canadian dollars, approximately £8,300, but we could stay in Britain and get easier fights for more money.

I'd knocked out four American fighters who had never been knocked out before. Although Jefferson Davis wasn't quite good enough to beat the best, it took something to beat him, and this was known the other side of the water. We were better set for a world title shot than we had ever been, and Jim said so one day to Leslie Grade, the impresario, in the Nightingale Club in Berkeley Square : 'I could show you the way to earn a lot of money. Henry is the only man ever to put Clay on the floor. Can you imagine an Englishman fighting for the heavyweight title in his own country? You wouldn't be able to buy the publicity.' Grade said, 'Well, Jim, we're not boxing promoters.' Jim said, 'if you want a man I can get you one.'

In March 1966 Ali beat Chuvalo on points to keep his world title and things were really hotting up for us. But these matches aren't arranged out of the blue. Over the transatlantic phone Jim spoke to Arthur Grafton, the Louisville lawyer who looks after the interests of the Kentucky millionaire group which launched Ali. They were interested but we had to wrap up an attractive financial package. Ali was declared eligible for military service but his call-up was deferred—in fact he had five more fights after me before he forfeited the title in 1967. Jarvis Astaire, of Viewsport (he specialises in closed circuit TV and cinema, and was closely involved in all the negotiations), television people, Arsenal Football Club, and so on, all had to be consulted so that Harry Levene, the promoter, could offer guarantees. We didn't want Wembley Stadium because they charged so much—£25,000 for an outdoor show there. It had to be an open air stadium where you could seat 50,000 people and the Arsenal directors offered very reasonable terms. So, the deal was finally clinched, after four months' negotiations, for the fight to take place at the Arsenal's Highbury Stadium at 9.30 pm on Saturday, May 21.

For me the purse and ancillary rights were going to add up to £50,000 and more. The contract was on a percentage basis but with a guarantee worked into it if for any reason the percentage did not come up to expectations. Jim never signed just for a percentage; he always demanded the guarantee. He wanted to be covered on whichever was the greater. Ali was getting a flat rate of £100,000 plus ancillary rights such as American and Canadian closed circuit television, and a percentage on all TV, radio and film rights. It was the most he got until he fought Joe Frazier in 1971. We had the rights for Europe and the Far East. Directly Telstar, the TV satellite, started to circle the earth, top boxing became huge business, and we were there at the right time. The fight was going to be in the cinemas of every major British city except London, with people paying between £2 and £5 a ticket. At Highbury, where a crowd of 40,000 was certain, they would be paying from 30s. to £15. But hundreds of millions were going to see it on their screens in places like Tokyo, Bangkok, Dortmund, Mexico City and Buenos Aires. It was a fantastic thought. And as the publicity boys weren't slow to point out, this was going to be the first world heavyweight title fight in Britain since Tommy Burns knocked out Jack Palmer in four rounds in 1908. The last British-born heavyweight to hold the title was Bob Fitzsimmons, from Cornwall, who beat James J. Corbett in 1897.

Our preparations and plan of campaign were not so different from before. We'd fought Ali once so we knew exactly what to expect. We knew he would again concentrate on speed, because I had hurt him and he would want to keep out of trouble. In the event he came in at his lightest, which showed he had trained hard and trained for speed. If you look at his career record you see he came in at his lightest for me on both occasions. Naturally, then, we got fast sparring partners, boys who could imitate his style. Training for speed means a lot of road work—you've got to have your legs as good as they can be. I knew I would have to chase him again. If I stood off and became a stationary target he would look a million dollars. If he boxes at his own speed you've had it. You've got to pin him on the ropes and in corners, cutting off the angles, to reduce his manoeuvrability. It's the only way you can beat him. Plenty of big guys have tried standing off him, but all they've done is make him look marvellous.

For the five weeks' training we arranged to spar daily at the Thomas a'Beckett gymnasium in the Old Kent Road, which we'd done since I started pro boxing, and live at the Duchess of Edinburgh at Welling with Bill Gardiner, 'our lucky camp', as Jim put it. Most boxers are a bit superstitious. Around midday we would drive up to the Thomas a'Beckett after the road work. I always drove myself because I could relax while driving. The promoters never objected; years before we had that out. They don't like you doing things like going up in light aircraft or horse riding, but I'd been driving in London for years and it was no more dangerous than crossing the road on foot. We ate the food I liked to eat, mostly good rare meat, salad and French dressing, and potatoes. It was only in the last week that I really controlled my diet. I liked to go into the ring empty, to be cleared right out.

Everything went as we planned in training. We knew exactly what we had to expect. On the early morning runs we met the same guys day after day. I'd got my own built-in alarm clock for waking at four in the morning. Danny had the next room, but I would always be awake five minutes before he came in to me. You got to know an early morning life which you shared with just a few regulars, and right pally you were with them. It's quite countrified around Welling, with plenty of open spaces, sports fields and paths. I was a familiar sight myself, jogging along followed by Danny on his bike, the sun just coming up. All the coppers knew us, and we'd see the same paper vans dropping the papers off at the shops day after day. A young boxer who used to be with Jim was on the lorries, and he would see us, flash his lights and shout 'Hullo, Henry. Keep it going, lad.' And the coppers would slow down in their cars, or pedal along at my jogging speed, asking me how things were going and what the chances were. Some would ask why we were out so early, why boxers did this. The answers are really very simple. If you are anywhere in the London area you need to be up on the road before all the cars start polluting the atmosphere. And the second reason is that you have to try and get enough rest period between the road-work and the gym. If you finish early you have got time to eat your breakfast, digest it and have a rest before the gym session at midday. So after I got up at four, did my running, sweated out and showered, I could be back in bed by 5.30 for two and a half hours more sleep and rest before breakfast. Then I could relax after breakfast until I travelled the few miles up to the Thomas a'Beckett.

With the fight taking place at 9.30 pm on the Saturday, we had our last sparring session on the Thursday. On the Friday I just did a light sparring session of four rounds. Some fighters like to have a complete rest for two days, but I preferred to keep the old circulation going. We went up to Sheekey's fish restaurant for lunch on the Friday for a change of scene, then it was back to the Duchess of Edinburgh for the last night before the big occasion. All the talking had been done by then. We'd got all our tactics laid out. I had a slightly later night on the Friday, watching TV until 10.30, a chat with Albina on the phone, then I went to bed and slept like a baby—getting to sleep never worried me. In a curious sort of way I hadn't really thought of the fight until the day actually dawned and I had to get ready for the weigh-in and the medical. All through training I knew it lay ahead of me, but the day-to-day routine was completely absorbing. I never looked ahead saying to myself supposing this happens or that, and wondering at the consequences.

On the day of the fight, though, things were a little different. George was with me for every minute of it, going right through the whole routine from early morning. When we got back from a walk after breakfast we sat down and played ten-card rummy for an hour. Then we lay on top of our beds relaxing. It was then that I began to think ahead. I knew a lot depended on me. People had been coming up to me in the street and saying, 'You can do it, Henry.' Or, 'Stop his old lip.' All that sort of thing, and from all sorts of people : ordinary housewives, old ladies in cars who used to stop, wind down the window and wish me luck—old dears, butter wouldn't melt in their mouths, or so you'd think. They might not be a bit interested in boxing normally, but here they were telling me to knock poor old Ali senseless, button his lip, do him up, all that sort of thing. I don't think it was colour prejudice. If he had been a white boy they would still have said it. Clay, or Ali as he called himself then, was a big mouth by American, let alone English, standards. He set out to make people hate him, to have people wanting to see him knocked out. It filled stadiums and it did things for him. He set a challenge for himself. I'm not discounting the colour aspect. Ali had a lot going for him after he joined the Black Muslims. Brother, some of those fellows were hard guys, and his black opponents knew it. But he could much more easily psych out a black fighter than a white. He had quite a lot of trouble against boxers like Jerry Quarry, and Karl Mildenberger, who after me took him to twelve rounds. The English just don't like big talkers. If you go on like Ali does there will be some in America who love you. But if you boast and say what you're going to do to your opponents over here in Britain they loathe you. This time he was going to knock me out, but he didn't say which round it would be in. He'd cut out most of his prediction lark by this time, although to one of the pressmen he did say he would be going for a clean KO. I had read our own press. They nearly all tipped Ali but I didn't expect otherwise. Lying on the bed, I thought of all the people hoping and expecting things of me, thinking to myself I would have to do my best for them. And I thought about my family, Albina and Henry Marco, and how marvellous it would be for them if I could win the world title. Fighters don't think defeat—at least I never did. If any fighter goes in thinking 'What am I going to do if he knocks me out?' then he is asking for the very thing he most fears. Every fighter must go into the ring thinking, 'No one is going to beat me.' And if you have trained well, and are not concealing any injury or ailment, then you must stand your chance.

A hire car firm put a chauffeur-driven Rolls-Royce at our disposal for the day. They told me, 'If you win we won't charge you, and if you lose it will only be half price!' Just before midday the Rolls called to take us to the weigh-in at the Odeon, Leicester Square. I'd seen Ali once before on this trip, at a press reception in town. We had shaken hands and he'd done his publicity bit, the old glare and all that. At the weigh-in, he was chipping and chatting on the scales, and then I had to stand next to him for the photographs. He was giving me the stare and nicking all the publicity, but as I looked at him right up close I noticed one solitary black hair on his chest. I said, 'Oh, look, he's a man all right, he's got a hair on his chest.' And I gave the hair a tweak. That brought the house down. They loved it. Ali didn't say a word, he didn't come back as he usually did. It took him right out of his stride. Then we went back to our respective camps, Ali to the Piccadilly Hotel—he was training at the

Boxing Board of Control's gym at the Noble Art on Haver-stock Hill—and the Rolls took us back to Welling. There we had our main meal of the day, a nice big rare steak, mixed salad and no cucumber or onions so they wouldn't repeat—I made that mistake once before. With it I had a couple of glasses of light red wine. I liked the lighter wines, claret or, an especial favourite, Fleurie sent up by Simpson's in the Strand. It was a beautiful light Beaujolais which we always had when we went to Simpson's.

We set off for Highbury in the Rolls-Royce at about 6.30 pm. We wanted to be there well before the fight, and we were going to pick up a police escort on the outskirts of Highbury. It was a good job we did, too, because when we got near the stadium there were thousands milling round. Everyone wanted to wish us well, and we would never have got through but for the motorbike outriders. It was fantastic. There were four of us in the car, Jim, Danny, George and myself. We just talked about ordinary things. We were all in good spirits, chipping and chaffing and keeping it light. No boxing talk at all. But the closer I got to the arena, and the bigger the crowds grew, so I found myself with slight butterflies in my stomach. I wasn't too keyed up. It was marvellous to see all those people and you could tell it was going to be a hell of a good gate. That matters to any pro-fessional! The police ushered us round the back of the stadium and then to the training pitch where we parked the Rolls. The police were very good to us. Afterwards, as we left, all the police who had been on duty that night—and there must have been more than two hundred—were gathered on the training pitch. We climbed into the Rolls thinking they weren't taking much notice, but, as we left, suddenly someone sang out, 'Three cheers for Henry.' And the whole lot of them took off their helmets and gave me these three ringing cheers. It's one of the great memories.

I was in the main Arsenal dressing-room and Ali was in the bums' room. I hadn't seen anything of him or his en-tourage and hadn't seen the arena even. But you could hear the roar of the crowd, and Jim and George went out just to have a dekko. 'Looks marvellous,' they told me, 'a wonder-ful crowd.' Most of the family were there. Mum, who'd only ever seen me box as an amateur, was out there. So was Albina, who'd never been to a boxing match before. The last thing I did before leaving Welling was to ring her up for a final word. Dad was there, and Bern and his eldest boy, Mark, who was thirteen; Bill Button, my cousin, who always followed us when we were in London; Tom Nutkins, an uncle on my mother's side, a tough old bird of seventy and a right cockney. When they played the National Anthem he stood there to attention with the tears streaming down his face. Any other time you could have hit him over the head with a bottle and he wouldn't have blinked.

Dad had been to all my fights in England and one or two abroad, and he was in the dressing-room, as usual, beforehand. Of course we had to limit the people there to my handlers and those closest to me. The four corner men were Jim Wicks, Danny Holland, George, and Johnny Shannon, who was looking after the water. Bern looked in, and so did our old friend Bert Marsh, and Jim Wicks's son, Jackie. Bert and Jackie were the biggest worriers out. On the television there are those scenes where a woman is having a baby and the husband is walking up and down the hospital corridor. That's how those two looked, hands behind their backs, up and down, Jackie walking one way and Bert the other. In the end we said, 'Here, do you mind!' If we'd had a carpet they'd have worn holes in it. They're great friends of ours, and they loved it, but on a fight night they were always dead nervous.

While I started to change Jim Wicks opened the telegrams. There were all the regulars, all the restaurants I visited regularly, like Simpson's and Sheekey's. Mrs Williams from Sheekey's never missed, and I would have been a bit upset if she had. Les and Ann Denny from the Bellingham pub, Richard Burton and Liz Taylor, Donald Houston —there were all sorts of people wishing me well. Jim would never let me open the telegrams or letters on the night because you do get the cranks. There was one guy who would be after me as regularly as clockwork after I first won the British title. He'd start by insulting Jim, then a reference to me, 'You big bub,' or something more obscene, and of course leave them unsigned. I just laughed and tore them up. I knew how to upset him all right! But there was nothing to upset us this night. George checked all my gear, although we'd been over it two or three times before we packed it. George also had to lay on the ice and the clean drinking water, and he would fill up the bottle, just an ordinary mineral water bottle, screw on the lid and then tape the mouthpiece and middle of the bottle so there was no chance of it slipping when it got wet. The ice packs are made of rubber, and George filled these and screwed on the lids.

Danny meantime cut the tapes provided by the Boxing Board of Control steward. We would need about nine three and a half inch strips to go across the hand, then a long piece of about eight inches which he would cut into three to go between the fingers. No two boxers tape in the same way. Taping is not to make your hand any harder so that you can knock your opponent out more readily, but to protect your hand. Before tapes were brought in fighters only used bandages, but they suffered a lot of injury because of the spreading of the bones of a hand with the impact of a punch. Tape stops the spreading. If there's too little it doesn't serve its purpose, but too much is bad because it restricts your circulation. Jim always believed in a boxer doing his own hands. If you buy a pair of shoes you don't ask the assistant if they feel comfortable. Only you know if they are or if they are not, and the same applies with the tape. That night, in the Highbury dressing-room, I taped as I had always done—I put the plaster against my skin in cross fashion, three slanting across the knuckles one way and three the other. Then I bandaged around the thumb and hand just below the knuckle. I put three strips through the fingers, and the tape I had left I bound around to keep it all in and to cover the knuckles. The steward stamped the hands with an ink stamp, and after that you couldn't add any more.

Of course you don't make the mistake of taping your hands before you've taken off your trousers and put your boots on! Taped in my left boot were religious medallions which people who meant a lot had given me. One was from Albina. Another was from Albina's aunt, Maria Rizzi. I would always tape these under the tapes which I put over the boot laces to stop them coming undone. Last of all I put my shorts on, and then I started warming up, shadow boxing and loosening up exercises. People came in to tell me how the other fights were going. Then the last fight before me . . . four rounds to go . . . three rounds. . . . There were the last few coming in to wish me well.

George Smith, the referee, came in with the main instructions. He is a good referee, and he understands the game. I knew him well but we went through the ritual. 'Well, good evening. I'm George Smith, the referee. I want a clean fight. When I say "Break" I want a clean break. I want both of you to take a step backwards. I want no rabbit punching. You must punch correctly with the knuckle part of the glove. I won't be scoring points if you're slapping. If one man goes down the other must go into a neutral corner, and I won't start counting until you're there. All the best, and may the best man win.' I'd heard it all before dozens of times, but they had to do their job. Onslow Fane, the president of the Boxing Board of Control, came in to wish me well, Teddy Waltham, the secretary, my old schoolmates Johnny Gibson and Jimmy Rushton, and Harry Levene, the promoter, who had been in to see Ali as well. Poor old Harry. Ali wouldn't sign the contract until he was sure he would get the largest ring available. Naturally, if you're a boxer fighting a puncher you want as much room as you can get. In Britain that meant a twenty foot square ring, but there just wasn't one that size to be had anywhere. Harry had it made specially, and it cost him £500. If there was no other reason, old Harry would remember Mr Ali!

I always said a little prayer before I left the dressing-room, and made the sign of the cross. I didn't say, 'Please let me win,' it was just asking God to watch over me and keep me safe, thinking really of the family. And you asked that you would be able to do your best and put up a good performance. There was a fantastic atmosphere building up outside. The fight immediately before ours finished and you could hear them all chanting, 'En-ner-ree! En-ner-ree!' The chief whip called me, 'Come on then. They're ready,' and then it was a few steps into a corridor, a right turn down gradually sloping steps, with Jim in front and saying 'Watch that step, careful there', and we were in the arena. Then the roar really hit me like something solid. There was a flag bearer out front carrying the Union Jack, then Jim, still mothering me to make sure I didn't do an ankle any injury, then George behind to stop people crowding me. Then we were in the ring, the lights were dimmed again and there was a fanfare for Ali. He got a good reception, a few cheer-ful boos of course, but the British public are usually very fair. Jim Wicks pulls two pairs of boxing gloves out of the box at the ringside, Ali's man does the same and while the gloves are going on the MC introduces celebrities like Richard Burton, Donald Houston and Stanley Baker. Then came the National Anthems, and as I stood there, for the first time I can remember in the ring I could feel a lump in my throat. With that finished there was another great roar, I looked quickly for Albina for one last wave to her, then the main floodlights went off and the spotlights concen-trated on the ring.

CHAPTER FIFTEEN

The bell rang, I was up and out of my corner as Muhammad Ali left his and suddenly the size of the ring hit me. It was just like the Albert Hall, big as a ballroom. Good God, I thought, what's this? It seemed like ten minutes before I got to the centre of it. You could have had three fights in there at the same time. And that wasn't the only difference from the first fight. Ali remembered I had a left hook all right. In the first clinch I knew what his game was. It was just like being in a vice. When I got near him all he did was grab me, and hold me as tight as he could until the referee said 'Break'. Then he pushed me hard and jumped back out of distance. We knew he'd be watching for the left hook, so we'd practised the right hand a little more. I had to try and kid him with a few rights which would make him forget the left hook, so I didn't try to throw too many in the first round. I was aiming just to jab, jab away, but in the first round I was short with the left. I couldn't reach him at all. But I hadn't warmed up, I wasn't caring too much. It was me doing all the forcing, and him going back, but I suppose we ended up about equal. He didn't land anything to hurt and neither did I. It was much the same in the second round and the third. He just wouldn't engage in any inside work. I was trying to get to the body, but he'd learned a lot about inside work. I couldn't rough him up as I did before. He would grab me and hold until the referee broke us up. He knew that this early in the fight the referee wouldn't start to get at him for it.

In the fourth round I started to reach him. Ali always slowed down slightly at this point, and I began to catch him with good, solid left hands. Once or twice the left hook missed him by a whisker. Once Ali protested to the referee, not for hitting on the break, as some people thought, but for a low blow. Some people said afterwards, 'Why didn't you go in and belt him?' But he was two or three yards out of distance. Directly I went for him he was in his boxing pose again.

There wasn't much between us again in the fifth round, but I was reaching him better. Then came the sixth round and the disappointment of my life. Immediately after the fight I swore that there was a clash of heads. I really thought it at the time. He threw a right hand as I was coming in and something hard hit me. In the heat of the battle I thought it was his head. Afterwards, looking at the film, I could see it wasn't. He threw a left and a right, and as he threw the right I also slung a punch. He shortened his right—Ali is either a long puncher or a flicker—and the effect was a chopping blow on my eye with the heel of his glove. The eye split wide open. It was the worst cut I ever had in boxing, deeper and longer even than in my first fight with him. Immediately after that landed our heads came together, which made me think at the time that the damage was from a butt. I knew at once it was a bad cut with the warm blood gushing on my body. I could feel it on my shoulders and chest; it was really blinding me. You can see from the film that he came right in like a tiger, landing as many punches on the cut as he could. The referee looked at the cut once and then allowed me to go on. But I copped one or two more on it and he just had to stop it. It was a hell of a disappointment because most of the good judges had me just a bit in front on my aggression. I'd landed more punches than he had and the fight was going more or less as we planned. We knew he would be like greased lightning early on and make me miss, but he was slowing all right just before the fight was stopped. I was led out of the ring with scarcely a sweat on. You don't mind losing if you haven't the ability to beat a man. You say, 'Fair enough, he knew too much for me.' But on the two occasions I fought him, Ali didn't know too much for me. It was a physical thing that let me down—having prominent bones and weak skin tissue round the eyes. I'm not trying to take anything from him, but that is my objective opinion.

Albina had seen scarcely anything of the fight, as I've said. She'd just sat there with her face cupped in her hands, hardly daring to look. When I got back to the dressing-room Danny knew it was a really bad eye and the Board of Control doctor said, 'Don't you do anything here except bandage it up.' And he gave Jim the phone number of a plastic surgeon at Guy's Hospital. We made an appointment for the following morning, and I went home for a few hours' rest. The worst moment comes when you are alone and thinking about things. That's when it gets you, and you feel the disappointment right deep down. I didn't mind losing fair and square, but I knew in my heart I was doing well. But never for a moment did I say, 'Well, that's it. I'm packing it up.' Most of the press were saying at this point that I should. But it wasn't for the first time in my career, and it was what went on in my own heart and mind that mattered. If I'd been fighting a mug then, yes, I might have retired. But I wasn't. Ali was the world champion, and he wasn't beating me on ability. So I thought, 'Why pack up? If I'm getting well paid for doing a job I know I can do, why not carry on?' So I went to the plastic surgeon the following morning with my mind made up about that. A plastic surgeon was the right expert, not because of his skill with facial cosmetics, but because of his stitching. Whereas an ordinary surgeon simply stitches the top layer of skin the plastic surgeon gives you a local anaesthetic round the eye, then stitches in two layers, first with fine stitches on the inside of the cut and then over the top. You hear and see much of what is going on but you don't feel anything.

Albina was very good about things. I told her Jim and I would be sitting down and talking it all out. I knew she really wanted me to give up, but she said she would leave it to me. 'I know you and Jim will do the right thing,' she said. I knew my world title chances were finished, but there was still a lot of money to earn in Britain and Europe. Besides, I now had a business which needed support from my boxing income.

In 1965 I had begun thinking to myself that I would not

be in the fight game for too many more years, and now was the time to look around for some other means of support. Like a fool I went into the greengrocery business with my head down. No one suggested it. The idea was entirely my own. It came up, strangely enough, at a hotel in Las Palmas where Albina, Henry Marco and me were on holiday. There was another fellow called Cooper in the same hotel, and people kept calling out Henry or Harry which made me look round. We got quite friendly, and eventually it emerged that Harry Cooper had a greengrocery stall in Holloway, and he was going to look at a shop in Wembley to see if he might buy it. He asked for my advice as I lived there, and I said it was a good position, right in the busy part.

I had no interest then, but after we got back the fellow he was going in with suddenly pulled out. Harry was disappointed, and I thought, well, it's right on my own doorstep. I was looking for something else to do. Why not go in and help this guy out? It was an empty shop when we took it over—it had been a gents' outfitters before. It was right on a busy corner—No 4 Ealing Road, on a corner of Wembley High Street. For the first nine months to a year it was a hell of a good business. The only trouble was that we never seemed to make a profit. Although it was taking nearly enough a grand a week we just couldn't seem to make it pay. One reason was that the overheads were so high. Greengrocery is a risky business. You have got to know how to buy and there are big pitfalls. You can spend a lot of money on soft fruits, for instance, and if the weather suddenly is stormy it can all turn on you. So you've got to buy wisely and sell quickly. When we overbought there was a tremendous amount of wastage, and that was the profit gone. It's a business with small margins, and with the large overheads you can easily find yourself in trouble. For instance our rent was £3,250 a year—£63 a week rent, and in addition there were rates, lights and wages for at least five. On a stall you are dealing with passing trade; in a shop you are building a clientele. You've got to humour them, and be polite. People would come out of curiosity, because we stunted quite a few pictures of me serving potatoes and tomatoes. But after a while it was no stunt. That business really needed me in there. I couldn't be just a sleeping partner. At first I would look in just a couple of times a week. In the end it was four or five times, and even Saturdays and Sundays. Meantime I was turning down publicity jobs elsewhere, some of which were for good money. Public appearances, opening shops, church bazaars, variety club luncheons, charity interests—I always regarded these as part of the job of being a champion; I enjoyed doing them and still do. Most of us are show-offs, given the chance, and when you are invited here and there to say a few words you are flattered. I had a marvellous following with the mums and kids. They always gave me tremendous support. I knew I was 'Our Enery' to a lot of people, and while you don't want to overdo the Cockney bit you don't mind letting everyone know that that's what you are, and you are proud of it. At this time I never wrote out speeches; it was all ad lib. If you have to talk for ten minutes to a quarter of an hour, then naturally you have to prepare and write a few notes down. But for the opening of a supermarket, say, I would just ask the guy if he wanted me to mention anything in particular, but other than that it would come straight off the top of my head. For a supermarket opening I might make 100 guineas; for a charity, such as muscular dystrophy, I wouldn't take a penny. But all this began to be affected by the demands the shop made on me.

We never bought at Covent Garden. We started off at Spitalfields and then we went to Brentford because it was quicker. Harry and me started by sticking in £500 apiece, but as the bills began to mount the creditors naturally began knocking at my door. I was the well-known name, so I was the man they mostly came to. Boy, I really had headaches! It was the only time I ever lay awake worrying. I had never owed people a penny in my life. Mum and Dad had brought us up to believe that owing money was wrong. To think that there were guys getting writs out for non-payments nearly drove me mad. But there was no way I could quickly get out. I couldn't have my name dragged through the courts, so I covered most of the debts. I hung on, trying to sell the place, but after getting people interested it would always fall through. Eventually I said, well, it's just got to come to an end. I've ploughed so much money in, but I can't stand it any longer. So just after Christmas 1968 I just pulled the shutter down on a loss of £10,000 and that was that. I paid dearly for that mistake, but on the other hand I had learned some lessons the hard way, and I remembered them when eventually I came to my retirement.

CHAPTER SIXTEEN

In 1966, there was I, thirty-two, still with a bit of boxing left in me, looking round for the kind of match which would not be too much of an anti-climax after Ali. There was still one world-class fighter around I had never fought, always by an unlucky turn of events, and suddenly he was available. The boxer was Floyd Patterson, world champion from November 1956 to September 1962 apart from the year when he lost his title to Ingemar Johansson. Patterson had made eight successful title defences before being knocked out in the first round by Sonny Liston in Chicago on September 25, 1962. In November 1965 Ali had stopped him in the twelfth round at Las Vegas, but three years later, in September 1968, he was to go fifteen rounds with Jimmy Ellis for the World Boxing Association version of the world title in Stockholm.

Should I take him or not? I was keen, but Jim Wicks was less so. Few people in boxing knew the weakness which had developed in my left elbow. Jim knew I could throw a left hook at a tall fellow, but when I tried it underneath the elbow gave me pain. Patterson wasn't a tall man as heavyweights go, and Jim reckoned I would have trouble landing the left hook over the top. For the same reason he would reckon to have by-passed Jerry Quarry in later years because Quarry is a relatively short man. Boxing is no game for weaklings or unfit men, and if there is something slightly wrong you have to conceal it well. If this had been widely known I would have been in more trouble. There would have been plenty of guys who would have tried everything they knew to strain the elbow, twisting or holding it in the clinches, that sort of thing. Sometimes it hurt but I couldn't let on. After a hard fight the elbow would seize up solid and I would need hot and cold compresses to get it loose again. But I wanted a go at Patterson, and my only regret is that I tackled the fight the wrong way.

Basically I had the know-how to beat him, but my mistake

was to try and fight him as I did Ali. Patterson was a counter-puncher so I should have said, 'You come to me.' But like a fool I took the fight to him, and though I did hurt him once or twice to the body I didn't connect to the chin. Then two minutes after the start of the fourth round Patterson caught me with one right in the whiskers. And it really was a good punch. I didn't see it coming, didn't feel it even. Suddenly the lights went out, and, seeing the film afterwards, I just fell flat on my face. If I had fallen any other way just possibly I might have got up. If I'd gone down on my shoulder or even my back I might still have been breathing properly and come to my senses that much quicker. But what with the punch and the fall—that was it. I was stone cold. Even when Johansson stopped me with that tremendous punch in Stockholm I was able to struggle to my feet, and my head was fairly clear although there was no strength in my legs. But this was a hell of a good punch, the cleanest and best I ever collected.

Patterson had faster hands than Ali. He was a fantastic right-hand puncher, hard and fast. He was not such a fast mover as Ali, but a far better puncher. In fact, technically he was a better fighter, but his mental approach was wrong. Patterson was the only man of my time who could put together eight or nine punches in a cluster, combination punches as they're more generally known, in a matter of two or three seconds. He's been known to clobber a man with one punch then compulsively hit him five or six times as he's on his way down. But his main enemy was himself. Mentally he was all wrong for the fight game. If he'd had the right temperament he would have been one of the greatest ever. To my mind he was too nice, too sympathetic to his opponent. Whenever he hit a man he always wanted to rush and pick him up. Any man who takes a black beard and dark glasses in his boxing kit and says to the promoter, 'Where's the back entrance so that I can get out quickly,' isn't really built for the game. Patterson was ashamed when he lost, but there's no shame in losing when you've given 100 per cent.

After my defeat by Patterson there were even more of the press boys wanting me to retire. Most of them were genuine in thinking I had had a good innings. I wasn't getting any younger and a lot of it was sympathy. They had seen me get this nasty cut eye with Ali, and there were several younger men coming up, Billy Walker and Jack Bodell, for example, who they thought might take my place. But the press men wouldn't give up their jobs if they were still getting good wages, so why should I give up mine? If Ali and Patterson had been mugs, then I wouldn't have needed the press to tell me to go. But one was a world champion and the other an ex-world champion and there was no disgrace in losing to either. I had the know-how and the knowledge to beat any of the youngsters in this country or Europe, so what was wrong with employing it? All cuts look worse than they are until they stop bleeding. I know sometimes I looked as if I'd been in a road accident. But you go and clean it up, a bit of adrenalin and a wipe-off, and you're yourself again. Retirement talk helps to sell newspapers, I suppose. My attitude to boxing was that it was my job, and whenever I went into the ring it was to get the job done as quickly and as efficiently as possible. At times I didn't have to look the best boxer in the world, even the best in Britain, or have the most sparkling technique, but as long as I could size a man up and then deal with him, that was the main thing.

I hadn't fought for the British title since beating Johnny Prescott in June 1965, and in the spring of 1967 we started to negotiate for a defence against Jack Bodell. The Patterson fight had been in the September of 1966. I'd had a good long rest, but I really needed a build-up fight. We decided to take Boston Jacobs, another coloured American, at the de Montfort Hall, Leicester, on April 17. Yet again, he was a real spoiler, and a hard trial horse. I was a bit too heavy, 13 stone 12, and I didn't box so well. He was thickset and strong, and I was too sluggish to deal with him as I should have done. I won on points over the ten rounds, but it was hard work. The one consolation was that I'd got over the eye. The surgeon had done his work well and there was no scar.

So it was Jack Bodell next, and the first time I had ever met him. He was having seven or eight fights a year, more than I would ever have wanted. He was twenty-seven, a good age for a heavyweight, and probably in his prime then. He'd had a good run on the Continent, no British boy had beaten him, and the Board had nominated him as my No 1 contender. The fight was on Wolverhampton

Wanderers football ground so he was very much the home boy. We knew from what we had seen and heard that he was about the most awkward southpaw you could wish to meet. He wasn't like Dave Charnley, say, who you could watch for two or three rounds without it hitting you that he was a southpaw. Charnley was stylish. But with Jack you only had to see him leave his corner and you knew he was a southpaw. He was all arms, gangling, no flowing movements. He trod on your toes, and your instep, he kneed you in the shin—I had three bruises as big as a penny where he caught me on the shinbone with his knee going in. You'd think he had a couple of nails in his shoes. He is just naturally an awkward guy, which was 70 per cent of his ability. Not that he was a dirty fighter. I've fought a lot dirtier fighters than Jack. He did it all unintentionally. When he trod on you, it was all accidental. If you were trying to back away from him, just as likely he would trip you up where he'd left his legs behind you. When you were on the ropes, you'd think, oh, I'll go this way, but then you realised he was still in range to catch you. It's a different way round, and it takes a bit of getting used to even for an experienced fighter.

In the first round we had decided just to feel him out. We knew Jack was an explosive starter, slinging punches as fast as he could in the first four rounds and quietening down afterwards. He came swarming out just as expected, and he was all over me, and though he wasn't catching me with his punches the crowd were going mad. Jack had only one way of fighting, and that was going forward, but while he was doing that he was leaving himself wide open. He wasn't a short, sharp puncher, he slung then from way out, and while he was doing that he could be hit. The classic way to deal with a southpaw is to counter with the right, but I found I could jab him or even catch him with a longish left hook, over the top of his right jab. In the first round I missed him with one or two good left hooks just by a fraction, so I came back to the corner and told Jim, 'Don't worry, I think I'll catch him all right.' And that is what happened. He came out exactly the same way in the second, but I caught him with a good left hook early on. He didn't go down, and I pushed him into the ropes and belted him. The ropes kept him up for a while, then he slumped over the middle rope and then right down, and the referee jumped in and stopped it. It was a calculation on my part. The crowd of 10,000 or so thought he was doing so marvellously, but it was only while I was sizing him up. With southpaws it's a matter of picking your opportunity and the right punch to finish things, not to look good yourself. They always bring you down to their level.

On August 5, 1967, John Pietro, my second son, was born, but Albina was scarcely back and the household getting used to having a baby around again than I was preparing for a fight with Billy Walker. I had seen Walker as an amateur on television, and he'd had one or two spectacular wins. In particular there was the famous occasion when British amateurs won all ten bouts against a team from America, and Billy had beaten a big coloured fellow called Cornelius Perry. Now Perry was undoubtedly the worst heavyweight boxer I have ever seen. He looked as if he was nine months' pregnant, and he must have weighed about seventeen stone. When he got in the ring you could see all that flesh bobbing up and down, and I can remember the commentator saying, 'Look at him, look how agile he is,' and thinking, 'Blimey, is he seeing the same man?' But Billy went in and did his job well, and so many million viewers saw it that he was made.

That one fight and the ballyhoo following it created 50 per cent of Billy's reputation. It was his undoing, really, because they paid him a lot of money for his first three fights—the contract was reported to be worth £9,000—and, naturally, Harry Levene wanted to put a bit of opposition in his way. That didn't help Billy, because he hadn't learned his trade as we had done. He went straight into eight round fights instead of six rounders. He was a game boy—any fellow who is prepared to take two punches in order to land one is game—and he always went into a ring 100 per cent fit. But he had to take a lot of punches, and in heavyweight boxing that means punishment. Billy in the end did the wise thing and got out at the right time, but it was a shorter career than it might have been, partly because of the extraordinary power of television.

For my fight with him at Wembley on November 7 my line of attack was not to try and knock him out straight away. He was a strong boy and you could hurt your hands on his head. I thought I would soften him up with a left jab for seven or eight rounds, then, if all went well, I could go to work on him later in the fight. And that's what I did. I pumped plenty of lefts, and unfortunately for him he had one of my old bogies in that fight, he had an inch-long slit over his eye. I saw it, Jim said, 'You know what to do,' and I did it. Boxing is a rough, tough business. I hit him with about thirty punches without taking one back, and the referee had to stop it. I reckon Billy was tiring badly by then and even without the cut I would have knocked him out in the next round. It gave me my third Lonsdale belt outright, and no one at any weight had achieved that in British boxing, but it did Walker's reputation little harm either. The boxing public generally are a bloodthirsty lot. They like to see a good hard fight, and if there's plenty of gore and snot flying around they love it. And they always got plenty of that with Billy. He'd have them up on their feet shouting. It's all back to basics. That was what they liked and he gave it to them. A hundred per cent value for money was Billy—game and strong without all that much ability and technique. It was exactly the combination that many of them wanted.

CHAPTER SEVENTEEN

In 1968 I had only one fight, on September 18 against Karl Mildenberger for the European title which they had taken from me in 1964, ironically when I couldn't fight Mildenberger because of an elbow injury. But it wasn't my elbow which troubled me in 1968 so much as my right knee cartilage. I'd been feeling this for the last couple of fights and in the training before then. I would have to be on the road for ten minutes before this nagging pain in the knee would go. I had cortisone injections and physiotherapy massage for it, and at the time it was put down to being a pinched cartilage. But I knew in the back of my mind that the trouble was likely to reappear.

What with that and the problems of the greengrocery shop, which was draining me of capital, the one consolation of the year was that fight with Mildenberger which brought me back the European title I'd never lost in the ring. The fight had gone to purse offers and Levene had got it at

Wembley, so Mildenberger knew he was on to a good thing. He had put up a pretty good fight against Ali in Frankfurt in 1966, though mainly, I think, because he was a southpaw. He took a bit of a belting in the thirteen rounds he went. I saw the fight on film and he was able to last that long only because Ali had a little more to fathom. Possibly Mildenberger was just over the hill, because he lost another fight in America after that.

He wasn't such an awkward southpaw as Bodell. He was about as tall as me, but heavier and thicker set. I went in at 13 stone 4½, a bit light, but the right weight for this fight. He had a bit of finesse, but you could anticipate what he was going to do, and I was able to move around him a bit. He was a box-fighter with a good knock-out record. The Germans, rather like ourselves, throw up most of their boxers from the big industrial towns. The Ruhr—Dusseldorf, Dortmund, Essen and so on—seems to be the home of German boxing, I suppose the harder working conditions creating the demand and the supply for boxing.

As fights go, this was a fairly easy one for me. I jabbed well, boxed well and felt good. Mildenberger was a good boxer for a southpaw. He had a fair right jab and for the first round it was touch and go. But after that I got on top and he started to use the head a bit. The Italian referee warned him a couple of times, then in the eighth he stopped the fight. There was a clinch and as we came apart there was blood over my right eye. As the referee was looking at my eye the bell rang, then the referee raised my arm. I believe some of the press at the ringside thought that the referee was invoking one of those rules peculiar to the European Boxing Union. This says that if a man is ahead on points in the second half of a fight and is then unable to continue because of an unintentional butt he becomes the winner on points. I was certainly well ahead on points. One report said the referee made it five rounds to me, one to Mildenberger and one even. Anyway, no one disputed the verdict, which was a stoppage for illegal use of the head. Mildenberger's corner I think were pleased for it to end at that point.

So, eight rounds at three minutes, seven intervals at one minute, thirty-one minutes all told, represented my boxing work for the year of 1968 so far as the public was concerned.

That takes no account of keeping fit and formal training, sessions with the physiotherapist and specialists and the various therapies. But in addition there was what I call my public relations. I took that very seriously and still do. It's a part of my job and a part of my income. TV commercials were big money. Jim Wicks would ask £1,000 or £1,500 for doing them, and then there would be repeat fees. At that time I did one for Crown paints which was very successful and worth a lot of money to me. It had a boxing theme, and everyone seemed to like it. Then I did one for plastic padding, and there were various others. I enjoyed making commercials and being on television. The more you do the more you get used to it, and you learn to relax in front of cameras. In the end, after sixteen or seventeen years of it, you felt an old hand. Going into a television studio was no strain at all. It was like walking into my own home. I could sit down and chat with an interviewer without any nervousness at all. If he was a young chap a bit new to his game you got to the stage where you felt you could help him out by being relaxed.

I'm not nervous in front of people. I hate to read a speech off a bit of paper, but if I have to address an important meeting or a luncheon or dinner where there will be five or six hundred people, and I know I have to speak for ten minutes, then I'll have some worries because that represents quite a few words. So I do some homework and I'll take a piece of paper with me as a help to my memory. Some people have a gift for after-dinner speaking. I haven't and it's hard work. A few minutes of ad lib, that's really me.

One of the most unexpected invitations I had about this time was to talk about boxing at Eton College. It also started a set of newspaper stories that 'Our Enery' was sending his boys to Eton, which was a little embarrassing. It all came about when I was asked to speak on the medical aspects of boxing. I took along Jim Wicks and an eminent surgeon, Arthur Dickson Wright, a great friend and very much a boxing supporter. I said there was no danger in boxing as long as it was supervised properly and you were properly fit. We met the headmaster and several house-masters, and that was how the press story arose. One of the house-masters happened to ask if I had ever thought of putting my elder boy down for Eton. I said , 'No', so he said, 'I'll send you some details.' When I got home I told Albina; she said, 'Oh, lovely,' and I wrote off. There were always a lot of pressmen in and about the house, and Albina happened to mention this to one of them. He blew it up out of all proportion. According to this I'd been invited to send my son to Eton. The house-master got on to me and he was pulling his hair out.

'Oh, Mr Cooper,' he said, 'I do hope you haven't misunderstood me. We didn't *invite* your son.'

'Look,' I said, 'I know that. This press guy is just making a story. He twisted my wife's words and got it out of proportion. My wife never said that.'

So it passed off. But otherwise it was an enjoyable experience. It was great fun talking to the boys. A week or two before they had Harold Wilson there. He was then the Prime Minister, but the place was half empty. They couldn't cram them all in when I went there, they were up to the rafters, which says something for boxing and the interest it creates, if not for me. I never seriously thought of sending Henry Marco there. The master was very kind to me in pointing out the procedures and I thought there was no harm in finding out. When I saw the fees I'd found out enough—nearly £1,000 a year. As they explained, a bricklayer's labourer can send his son there if he has the money and the boy passes the entrance exam. But they don't invite anyone, not even Royalty, which of course I understood.

In general the press and television commentators are pretty good to the game. There are one or two knockers in the press but if you don't like something and don't agree with it then why go and watch it? There's one journalist nearly always at the ringside and yet he is always knocking the pro game. It doesn't make sense to me, except that he just has to be a controversialist. The majority of the established boxing writers and commentators know what they are talking about. One or two are nonentities—what they know about it me and two million others have forgotten. But there aren't too many like them.

CHAPTER EIGHTEEN

If 1968 was a mixed-up year, then 1969 often seemed completely crazy. It began marvellously with the announcement in the New Year's Honours List that I was to be made an Officer of the Order of the British Empire. The same month, January, brought the offer of a world title shot against Jimmy Ellis, the coloured American, in the autumn, providing I kept my European title against Piero Tomasoni in Rome during March. In May I turned in the British championship in protest at the British Boxing Board of Control's failure to support me over the recognition of the fight with Ellis for the world championship. For the second time the European championship went by the board, and finally, after a cartilage operation, I needed all the help that Arsenal, the most generous of football clubs, could provide to get me fit for a comeback which some people thought was beyond me.

The announcement of the OBE doesn't come as a complete surprise because they have to find out at some stage beforehand whether you are willing to accept the honour. A week or two before Christmas someone from Downing Street contacted Jim Wicks. Of course we were only too pleased to accept but we were asked not to tell anyone except family. When I broke the news to Albina she thought I was joking. She just refused to believe it. 'Straight up—it's true!' I said, and we had to start thinking of the things I would need to wear for the investiture. It turned out to be something of a sportsmen's Honours List. Chris Finnegan, who had won a boxing Gold Medal at the Mexico Olympic Games, was awarded the MBE, so were David Hemery, Bob Braithwaite, Rodney Pattison and Iain Macdonald-Smith, who also won Gold Medals in 1968. Then there were Ann Jones the tennis player, David Bryant the world lawn bowls champion, and Tony Nash and Robin Dixon, the bobsleigh Gold Medallists of 1964.

The investiture was on February 17, and the day before I went to Moss Brothers in Covent Garden to hire full morning dress. The right dress for an investiture is slightly different from what you wear to Ascot or a wedding, although a lot of people do go like that. But Moss Brothers made sure I was wearing exactly the right things, with black topper—not grey—and a black morning coat with pin-stripe trousers. I surprised myself. I looked very smart. There was no trouble about size. I was in a pretty fortunate position of being champion and all that and well known. The little perks are handy. When I went to 'Moss Bros' the manager knew me and I had his personal attention, so I was sure everything would be just right. They got me the correct gear, looking it up in the book to make absolutely sure. I had a nice new topper and a suit that had never been worn before. They did me up looking like a million dollars. Shoes, shirt, tie, everything was laid on, though they had a bit of trouble with a $17\frac{1}{2}$ shirt. All this for about a fiver. When I got home I unpacked it all, showed it to Albina and Henry Marco and then we hung it up. I had a Bentley at the time, and the following day I drove Albina and Henry Marco to the Palace—you are allowed two relatives or friends in the investiture hall.

Albina looked a treat in a black mink coat I'd bought her for our ninth wedding anniversary, a black hat with pom-poms from Fenwick's of Bond Street (specially for the occasion) and the black and white dress she had for John Pietro's christening.

At the Palace gates there was the usual bit of chipping from the coppers, 'Well done, Henry,' that sort of thing. I dropped Albina and Henry at their entrance and I joined one hell of a crowd—knights, OBEs, MBEs, about four or five hundred people all in different waiting-rooms according to their honours. I was in a bit of a daze; I didn't really recognise anyone, although several people I know came up to me afterwards and said they were there.

We seemed to be waiting in galleries, beautiful galleries hung with fabulous oil paintings. You could see all the famous names, Tintoretto and such people, and I can remember trying to guess how much they must be worth. On these occasions you wish you could go through it all a second time. The first time you are so excited and tense that you can't really capture it and savour it for your memory. It was the same when I went to the Palace for lunch. People afterwards ask you for the details, but it all seems to go so quickly that you can only give them a few impressions. It's marvellous, but if only you could relax a little more! You are called in according to order, the higher ranks first. They tell you what you have to do when your name is called. You go to a side entrance of the investiture hall, and as your name is called you walk towards the Queen. You turn left, you bow, you walk two paces forward, you bow again and receive your award, and the Queen has a few words with you. You mustn't turn your back on the Queen, so you take two paces backwards, you bow again, you turn again and then you walk off. You're naturally a bit tense, hoping you are going to do it right, and it's surprising the number of people who stand up to an army or a screaming audience without batting an eyelid who yet make little boobs at an investiture : turn the wrong way, turn their backs on the Queen, forget to bow or something.

It was marvellous when I walked on. The Queen looked round straightaway as my name was called and she smiled a wonderful smile as I walked towards her. She knew about my boxing, because at the time I had been having knee trouble and she asked me about it. I told her it was a lot better and I was back in training, and she said, 'It's marvellous to see you again,' because I had met her on one or two other occasions. The Queen spoke to me longer than to anyone else according to Albina, but she's a bit biased, I can't help thinking, and since she'd been ten minutes late at the restaurant where we all met up beforehand — Jim was in a right panic — it was perhaps a bit of conscience.

There has always been plenty of variety in my life, but from Buckingham Palace to the Palazzo della Sport in Rome was about as big a jump as you can make. The only thing they have in common is the palace bit. I defended the European title there against Piero Tomasoni, the Axeman of Manerbio, on March 13. It was the roughest, toughest fight of my career. Although Italy was Albina's home I had never fought there before. On holiday I had met a few boxing people, and I'd been to a professional show and got the atmosphere. At least I thought I had, but nothing in my career prepared me for the scenes there. Nor were there any signs of trouble at the start. The crowd gave me a good reception. In the build-up to the fight Albina had been interviewed at home by a number of Italian pressmen—naturally she had to tell them that although Italian born she would be over the moon if I knocked out Tomasoni in the first ten seconds! Anyway the crowd applauded me as I left the dressing-room and in the ring gave me a colossal cheer. Albina's family didn't come. They were a long way from Rome and, being country people, they had animals to feed and just couldn't disappear for a day. They had followed the preliminaries through the papers and they saw the fight on TV in the local bar. I think all the villagers there were shouting for me! When Tomasoni started to hit me below the belt, they were all shouting 'Sling him out', so Albina's mother wrote later.

Tomasoni was a crude, rough fighter. 'Axeman' was about right. He could swing a long, looping right-hand punch in just the way a man swings an axe. He'd knocked out Bodell in three rounds at the Albert Hall so we knew he could punch. It was a dangerous right hand all right, but it was obvious. He was a strong, rough handful, but a class below Mildenberger. In the first round I knocked him down with a good left hook. He got up after a count of eight and, in fairness to him, he may not have known too much of what happened after. No mistake, this was a brawl, not a fight. In the second round he just punched anywhere. One of the punches landed so far below the belt it dented the cup over my genitals, and I was down on my knees. I'd never been hit so low in all my life, but there was the Dutch referee, Ben Bril, counting over my head!

A boxer's belt or foul cup is an aluminium alloy convex cup covering the genitals. It attaches round the hips and under the crutch, with rubber sponge below your belly button. If you get hit lower than that, right between your legs in the middle of the foul cup which actually covers your genitals, then it's mighty painful and could incapacitate you. To get hit there the blow has to be very low, a good seven inches below your belly button. It's got to be in between the legs. If you get hit at the top of the belly it doesn't hurt much because your muscles are strong and you've got the foam rubber protection. When I took that belt off after fighting Tomasoni it wasn't convex, it was concave! He'd hit me there three times dead centre. If he'd been off centre by a fraction I would have had bruises on my groin, but there weren't any. He was just bashing at the cup, and I've still got it upstairs at home to prove it. It's quite a keepsake, but not one I'd like to put with the cups in the sitting-room. It was the first time in thirteen years that it had been damaged in a fight. If the referee had warned him the first time it would probably have been all right, but Tomasoni just carried on. Fortunately I got over the pain of the first blow and went to work on him with the left—it was one I really felt I had to finish. In the fourth I hit him with another left hook and as he went down he grabbed me and pulled me on the floor. As I got up he hit me on the cup again. The fairground wasn't in it. The referee warned Tomasoni, and then the crowd decided to let rip. I didn't know whether they were having a go at me or him. Suddenly they started to roar and all of a sudden big blood oranges came whistling down. Poor Peter Wilson, the *Daily Mirror* boxing columnist, who was sitting at the ringside touch-typing, had the biggest blood orange imaginable plodge right on the side of his face, and it nearly knocked him out. Jim and George saw this and then, as I went to sit in the corner, down came oranges, bread rolls and salami pelting into the ring.

I wasn't so much worried by the food. I was just waiting for the backs of the seats to follow. In an arena like the Palazza della Sport with a balcony fifty feet up they could knock you sparko. I was all ready for a quick dive under the ring. In the fifth round I hit Tomasoni with another left hook and after I'd struggled free of him he just slumped to the floor. He tried to get up but that was it, thank God.

A Rome crowd is perhaps something special. After the verdict they gave me quite a good reception so I don't think they blamed me for the brawl. British spectators are fairly knowledgeable about dirty tactics. They don't miss very much, but most dirty stuff is done on the blind side of the referee and sometimes the spectator, depending where he is sitting, gets a better view of it. I've had some blokes, mostly American, come at my eyes, literally gouging with their thumbs. They do it in a clinch so that your eye smarts and waters and you are temporarily blinded. Once or twice it has been so bad that I've had to say, 'Come on, ref, watch it . . . he's gouging.' Another nasty little trick some of them have is to rub the inside of the glove up the front of your face. Although the gloves have stretch elastic over the laces this can hurt a lot. Another dodge is to hold the back of the neck so that you can pull the head down on to the punch. I'm no saint and that was a favourite little trick of mine against some opposition. The bigger men tend to lay on, that is, use their weight to shove you around. The answer is for the lighter man not to react and try to push the other guy off. That is simply using up strength. If a big fat guy pushed me around I would let him until the referee stopped it. Another thing a heavy man would do was to trap you on the ropes and try to bend you over backwards. The referees are up to most of it, but on the blind side a lot can still go on. Some referees don't want to see it, and others don't even know it's going on. It's a part of the game and if you are a professional you've got to learn to cope.

José Torres, the former world light-heavyweight champion, who is making quite a name for himself in the USA as a journalist and author, has said that sometimes he let a boxer feel his pain, particularly after a punch to the liver. I was good on that punch, but I can't say I ever let a man feel pain consciously. To finish a man as quickly as possible was more credit to me than to let him suffer. Body punches can injure, and the pain lingers. But a good punch to the jaw is the best one really. I would throw a left hook to the liver or solar plexus just to get the guard down so that I had a clear shot at the chin.

Anyway, having survived in Rome, now for Ellis. Or so I thought. But once again life played one of its crueller tricks. Three months later I could possibly have been world champion. Instead I wasn't even the British titleholder. The harshest decision ever made by the British Boxing Board of Control about a British boxer ruined my chance of a fight with Ellis and left us no alternative but to renounce the championship I had held for ten years.

CHAPTER NINETEEN

On April 28, 1967, Muhammad Ali refused to join the American armed services and soon afterwards the World Boxing Association and the New York State Athletic Commission announced that Ali was no longer world heavyweight champion. Three months later the WBA announced a series of eliminators to pick their next champion, but Sonny Liston was not included and Joe Frazier refused to take part. All the best fights were going on outside the ring. Ali was entered in a computerised tournament and was beaten by James J. Jeffries and he then sued the Florida corporation responsible for a million dollars because it was a 'low blow to his reputation and prestige'. The WBA and the New York Commission were as usual having a set-to, the WBA nominating Ellis as their champion after he had beaten Jerry Quarry and Buster Mathis in their eliminators. The New York Commission refused to recognise this and named Joe Frazier. Well, forty-five American States were behind the WBA, together with the majority of other countries, and when Ellis's connections offered us a title shot that seemed good enough for us. But because our Boxing Board of Control had some agreement with New York, who have what they call the World Boxing Council as their international front, our Board refused recognition of my fight with Ellis as being for the world title. Their support for an American body, whose motives were as financial as everybody else's, they valued more highly than their support for me. And this was in spite of the small fortune they had taken from me to help keep themselves in being. Jim and I thought it a scandal and in May 1969 I gave up the British championship in protest.

A lot of people thought we were ill-advised. But Jim had been my manager for all those years and we had confidence in each other's judgment. The British Boxing Board of Control were quite prepared to call it a final eliminator, and next day they would have been knocking at my door for their money, which would have been a big chunk of my earnings. The British Boxing Board of Control earned more out of me than any other British professional boxer—any other three British boxers. They allow you 20 per cent for training expenses—with a £1,000 limit—then they are entitled under their rules to take five per cent of the rest of your purse and ten per cent of ancillary rights for all top-of-the-bill fights. Our expenses would run to a lot of money, £800 for hotel bills without sparring partners, trainer and corner men. All told it was more likely to be £3,000. Jim had to fight like hell to get the Board to lift their £1,000 limit for us, otherwise we would have been paying the five per cent on at least £2,000 unavoidable training expense. As it was, their five per cent represented big money. In the case of the Ali fight alone it was £11,000 for the pair of us, yet when I needed them they wouldn't support me. We talked of holding the fight with Ellis for the WBA title in Rome or Dublin, but cartilage trouble really hit me in training and that was the end of it. I also gave up my European title.

The operation took place at a Harley Street clinic, and a painful thing it was. When I asked for all the details, the surgeon said I must not be afraid to ask for pain-killing injections when I came round. I thought, 'He's trying to put the frighteners on me!' But, boy! you can understand how footballers dread it. I had the internal cartilage on the right knee done, but any operation where they have to dig round is painful, and I certainly needed those injections. There are two schools of thought on post-operative treatment. One says keep it moving, which means that five or six days afterwards you are getting some exercise for it. In my case they said I must lie quite still for a full fortnight. And I must say it paid dividends because I have never had a scrap of trouble since. I'm not saying it proves the case, but I've known people who got up quickly having more reaction.

Afterwards, the surgeons and doctors who attended me recommended that I should get my fitness back with Arsenal, who were used to my sort of situation. They knew over at Highbury what exercises to give, and how quickly to keep the recuperative treatment moving. After being on my back in hospital for two weeks I lost two inches on my thigh muscle girth because of the wasting. So I had to build that up again as well as strengthen my knee. Bertie Mee, the Arsenal manager, and George Wright, the trainer, were marvellous. Bertie was the one who had invited me to join them, and I went every day, Monday to Friday. Once I could do the exercises properly I trained with the players. At first I kept company with Bob Wilson, the goalkeeper, who had broken his wrist and had to get the use of it back. He's a great fellow, and we got very chummy. I would concentrate on my leg, lying down then sitting up with a sandbag across my ankles. That way I slowly got my strength back, and I also did some weight-lifting. We were either at the training pitch at London Colney or Highbury, and it went on for nearly four months.

If I couldn't have been a professional fighter I would love to have been a professional footballer. I was keen on football as a kid and to go to a team like Arsenal must be terrific, because the facilities there are outstanding. The young kids they sign never touch a broom. They don't waste their time being part-time sweepers or boot cleaners. There are four or five teams with the footballers training really hard. It surprised me just how hard. The days when they went to the ground a couple of times a week are over. They train almost every day and they really go through it. Their 'circuit training' almost finished me. Every week they had to lift so many weights, jump so high or so long, run this distance and that and so on; all in a certain time. They kept a record and had to keep trying to beat their best performance. It was all much more technical than I had imagined football training to be. In some ways I was like a fish out of water. Each sport requires different muscle training, and most boxers are developed from the waist up whereas most footballers are developed from the waist down. We're punching where footballers are turning, twisting and running.

With some of the running exercises I was finished halfway through. From the front of the main Arsenal stand to the very back is about fifty yards up steep steps. They time the boys to sprint up and walk back. No sooner are they down than they have to sprint up again. They have to do that ten times, but my lungs were bursting after eight. There was plenty of chit-chat and fun among the players. Charlie George was the only real Cockney in the team and they would nobble him because of his long hair. It was still a novelty at the time, and they used to sing out, 'You go first, darling,' and things like that. But it was a marvellous atmosphere and I was very sorry when Don Howe, the assistant manager, and George Wright left for West Bromwich Albion in 1971 at the end of the season when Arsenal won the double of F.A. Cup and League Championship. You can't blame them wanting to better themselves, but it is always sad to see a winning bunch break up. I was always impressed with the togetherness there. Everybody was Arsenal. Even the office cleaner and the guy who looked after the boots and equipment would get the chance of a trip abroad to one of Arsenal's European matches. I'm still a great Arsenal supporter, although I don't get the chance to see them as much as I would like. I'm pretty busy in the winter on Saturday afternoons, which of course is the chief day for fairs, fetes and the opening of this, that, or the other. But if I get the slightest chance I'm off to Highbury. Millwall and Charlton were closer to Bellingham, but I've had a soft spot for Arsenal from my younger days.

It was about this time that our own team suffered a breakup. Danny Holland, my trainer since I started professional boxing, left us, and it created a sensation in the boxing world. Just as it was with Arsenal, so it was with us : no one is happy when a winning team breaks up. I got on very well with Danny for most of our time together. Danny ran the gym and I was close to him, but I was even closer to Jim, who was doing all the arrangements and who was earning me my money. Over the years a bit of feeling built up between Jim and Danny. It all boiled down to what we paid Danny. We never signed him up on a percentage of my purse money, but we always looked after him well. Other trainers might be getting ten per cent, but they were getting ten per cent of peanuts. I was earning thousands, and Jim said Danny couldn't expect ten per cent of that. Jim would get mad when Danny kept on about percentages. Danny was getting about four or five thousand a year, which made him the highest paid trainer in Britain. The final break came just before my second fight with Jack Bodell; I was due to challenge Jack at Wembley on March 24, 1970, for the British heavyweight title, which he won after I'd renounced it the previous summer.

On the Friday before we were due to set up camp, Danny rang Jim to say he wasn't going unless he was paid more money. Jim told him if he wasn't satisfied he had better go somewhere else. Danny said, 'All right, I will.' And that was how it ended after fourteen years. Danny was a betting man, and so was Jim. But where Jim could lose hundreds of pounds on a race it never showed in his behaviour. Easy come, easy go ! If Danny lost a tenner, though, he'd come into the gym with a face as long as a fiddle. I'm not much of a betting man. If I bet at all, which isn't often, it is a pound top whack. One day I did go to the races with Jim and he put seven tenners on a horse. So I said, 'All right. I'll have a fiver on it.' Jim nearly fell through the floor, and the horse actually won. It was a good price and I got something like £40 back, but it didn't give me the bug. I'd sooner have the money in my pocket than give it to the bookmakers. I suppose Mum and Dad taught me that originally. They couldn't afford to gamble, but I don't think they would have been gamblers with a lot more money.

Now we had to look round for a replacement, and without much notice. What I wanted above all was a really good cut man, which was Danny's most important function with us. By now I trained myself to all intents and purposes. Jim and I talked it over and finally we decided to approach Eddie Thomas. Eddie was just finishing boxing as I started. I remember listening to broadcasts of his fights when I was a kid. He was British welterweight champion in 1949 and 1950, and Empire and European champion too. He became a successful manager, particularly of Howard Winstone, with his headquarters in Merthyr Tydfil. So we had known him for years, he was a good cut man, and he was happy to join us for the money we offered.

If I had fought Jack Bodell a second time with me still title-holder the fight would have been worth two bob. As it was, with Jack champion and me trying to win it back Wembley was a sell-out on March 24. I had been without the title for nine months and Jack had held it for five, having beaten Carl Gizzi, the Welshman with an Italian name. There was no quibble from the Board. How could there be? I went into this fight determined to take back a title which I thought was rightfully mine. I also wanted to give the right knee a thorough testing. I won fairly comfortable, though it was over fifteen rounds—the first time I had gone the full distance for more than six years—and the first time for nearly three that I'd gone more than ten rounds. I didn't stop Jack because winning a championship gives a man something, and he was a trickier proposition than he was the previous time. He didn't rush in and leave himself exposed so much. Going the full fifteen in fact gave me a lot of satisfaction. The knee felt good, and I was glad to know that at thirty-five, nearing thirty-six, I could still go the full time with a younger man. The scoring by George Smith, the Edinburgh referee who was in charge of the world title fight with Ali, was $74\frac{3}{4}$ to $72\frac{1}{2}$, which means that if each round was won by a quarter-point I took ten, Bodell three and two were even. So I was champion again, with more supporters, it seemed, than I ever had.

CHAPTER TWENTY

Of course by now I well realised that as a boxer I was past my prime, and that I had only a couple of good fights left in me. The game is always full of surprises though, and there were a few left for me. It was a pleasant one first. I enjoy being in the public eye and I can't understand people who seek publicity at one time, then try to shun it at others. But even with that sort of attitude I was completely taken by surprise when, one night early in 1970, I suddenly had a shove in the back and there I was on a Thames TV stage with Eamonn Andrews saying, 'Henry Cooper, this is your life.' I say completely taken by surprise but I think I have to qualify that. For a couple of weeks I knew something was going on but I couldn't put my finger on it. I would be due to meet Jim Wicks as usual when he would ring up and say, 'Sorry, can't see you today, I've got to meet a feller.' Well, I'd known Jim like a father for sixteen years and he would never talk like that normally. He'd say, 'Well, I won't be able to meet you because I've got to see Johnny so-and-so.' When he said, 'a feller', it didn't sound right somehow. He was being evasive, and so was Albina. About three days before it was screened, the phone rang, Albina answered it and talked away to someone very softly. When I came into the room she suddenly talked out loudly and quite differently. I tackled her about it. 'Look, what's all this about? It isn't *This is Your Life*, is it? Has Eamonn Andrews been on to you?' And she acted so well. She flew up in the air. 'It's nothing of the kind. Oh, you're so conceited. Look, I'll ring up ITV if you don't believe me.' She actually went and started dialling before I stopped her. 'Sorry, darling,' I said. 'I've got the wrong end of the stick.' I told her Jim had been acting a bit peculiar, and I thought something must be going on. But she really convinced me that I was imagining things, and I forgot all about it.

Then Jim rang to say that Liam Nolan, a sports broad-caster, wanted to do a recording on our views on all the British heavyweights. He was the front man, and he got on the phone and said, 'Henry, I want you to do this pro-gramme and can we meet in town?' He had a car laid on to take us to the studio, and while we were travelling he was asking me questions about this boxer and that, and he was saying, 'Yes, we'll use that.' He made notes and ran through various questions he would ask me, and I was quite con-vinced. In the morning Albina had told me she was going shopping. I saw she had a dress with her, and I said, 'What on earth are you taking that for?' She said, 'Oh, I've got to have it altered.' And I *still* didn't tumble. They had secret signs. If someone from the programme happened to ring up Albina and I came in, they had it all worked out. They had code phrases so they would know I was there, and they would ring off. It was all done very cleverly.

Anyway, when we got to the studio they said, 'Come on, this way.' But Jim Wicks wanted to know where the toilet was. 'It's back there,' they said. We were right at the door at this point. Jim stood back, the door opened and suddenly I'm shoved in the back and I'm through the door. Then I saw Eamonn, and directly I did I said, 'Would you believe it—you crafty old so-and-so.' All this had been going on for two months, so I found out later, and I was suspicious only the once.

I'd met Eamonn many times before, of course. He first made his name over here as a boxing commentator, and I'd often spoken to him on radio and television. There was a programme on television once where they showed you a bunch of kids and a set of personalities, and you had to guess which child belonged to which parent. My eldest boy, Henry, was there, and so was Eamonn with his little daughter. My boy goes over to Eamonn's daughter and says, 'Don't you worry. Just relax!' He wasn't ten years old at the time.

All the family were there for *This is Your Life* except Mum, who was going through a bad time. She'd had a slight stroke, she was a diabetic and on top of that she had flu. So thinking that the excitement would be a bit much for her she stayed at home and watched it on the box. Of the family, Albina, Dad, Bern and George appeared, and the kids from our home at Wembley. Another marvellous surprise was Ali, speaking from Cleveland. 'Henry,' he said, 'You're not as dumb as you look. I've never been hit so hard in my life.' I think one of the reasons Ali started to become much more popular in Britain was that he said the odd good thing about me.

It was nice to see all the old faces on the show. There was the man who first started me in boxing, Mr Hill. We never ever called him anything else except Mr Hill, and for the first time I knew he was Bob. He was seventy-six, and I hadn't seen him for over twenty years, but he seemed to look much the same as he did when we were kids. Then came Mick Cavanagh, the sergeant-major I'd put on the seat of his pants when I was seventeen and he was thirty-four. Then I met a few boxing mates—Jack Bodell, Billy Walker, Dick Richardson and the first guy I ever fought, Harry Painter. Poor old Harry. He'd lost more hair than me. Then they brought on a young amateur boxing kid called Archie Mc-Ateer. He had written to us from Preston and we had invited him to stay at the training camp for a few days. He loved boxing, and he would train with us in the gym and join in the road work. He was a bit young, and I had to tell him he wasn't ready for such hard work. But he was a nice kid, and mad keen.

These were good years for being in the public eye. For the second time I was made BBC Television Personality of the Year and I also won the *Daily Express* Sportsman of the Year award. I even helped pick Miss World in 1969. A lot of people think there is a fix to it. But there isn't, except that you are obviously not going to pick all the European girls and leave out the coloured ones, or vice versa. You're expected to try and get a cross-section if you can. They told us the main moment when to judge them was when they came out in their swimsuits. It was no good a girl having a flat chest and skinny legs even if she looked a million dollars in a dress. Of course if she had neither, but had flair and personality, and still looked good in a dress, naturally she would be one of the favourites. That time I had the winner, the Austrian girl, in second place. The girl I thought should win, Miss Czechoslovakia, didn't even get in the last seven. She had short hair, and I thought she was beautiful. But when she didn't make the final seven I went for the Austrian girl.

Of course they're all nice looking girls, but some capture your attention more than others; those, usually, who are not too nervous and tense. They are able to present themselves naturally, as if they are enjoying themselves.

Being on television a lot, chairing a sports panel for example, made me known to a whole new generation of children who probably had never seen me fight, even on television. I was always touched by the number of people, complete strangers, who would send me little remembrances or good wishes. I've had lots of paintings sent. Some of them could have been of anyone, mind you. But there is one story of a young fellow who was a great fan of mine. He was a miner who came from the North-east to watch most of my fights. I never knew him, but through the post one day came a little parcel. Inside was a hard-boiled eggshell, and on it, in lacquer paint, was a portrait of me wearing a Lonsdale belt all done in beautiful colours. On the other side of the egg all my titles were listed. It was a little masterpiece, because this fellow was a talented miniature artist. He had intended to give it to me at my next fight. Of course I knew nothing about this, but he meant to ask to see me in my dressing-room. Tragically, three days before the fight, he died in a pit accident. His sister knew about the egg and sent it to me through the post, with a letter which said, 'You were his idol. He thought so much of you. I'm sure he would want you to have it.' Unfortunately the egg got cracked in the post, and when the air got to the inside it really started to smell. So as best I could I cut out the white and the yolk, carefully scraped the inside of the shell, which was a tricky job because of the cracks, and stuffed it with cotton wool. I stuck it together as well as possible and it is still among the cups and things we have on display in the sitting-room. We wouldn't ever get rid of it. I wish we could have met the lad.

CHAPTER TWENTY-ONE

Towards the end of 1970 the possibility of a match with José Urtain, the Spanish holder of the European championship, began to be discussed. Who first thought of it I don't know, but Harry Levene wouldn't be thanking him over-much. True, Harry got his man in the end and presumably made a reasonable profit, but he paid for it. That match cost him more time, energy and chasing round than any he made for me. I had given up my European title the year before because of my cartilage injury. The EBU require you to defend your title every six months, and if I hadn't turned it in they would have stripped me of it. But we had an understanding from them that we would be given a chance to regain it at the first opportunity after I was fit.

Urtain was a colourful character. He came from the Basque country around San Sebastian where one of their main sports is rock lifting. Urtain was a champion at this, so was his father, and by all accounts his grandfather could lift a mountain. So we knew he was a well-muscled, shortish fighter, very strong, with a powerful right-hand punch. He hadn't beaten very much, his best being Peter Weiland of Germany for the title, and a points victory over Jurgen Blin, though many judges thought the German won. Urtain was basically a slugger with this good right-hand swing, if he connected. I wasn't especially apprehensive, though I was thirty-six and he was twenty-seven. The knee had stood up well to training and to the Bodell fight. I would sooner fight a man who had only one way of boxing, a big swing you could get inside, than the craftier guys.

Harry Levene offered Urtain more money than any foreign boxer since Ali. He was guaranteed £41,000 plus a share of ancillary rights which in this case were about £30,000. It brought his take to near enough £50,000, but there was a hell of a ding-dong before Harry could get him to sign. Harry still winces every time you mention his name, and in fact I think he overpriced the fight. He was paying Urtain too much. But that didn't stop a real pantomime as he chased him all over Spain trying to get his signature. One minute Urtain was in Madrid, and Harry would dash off there, only to find he was somewhere else. In the end Levene got so frustrated he wanted us to sign to meet Blin on the same date while asking the EBU to strip Urtain of his title. But that might look as if we were running away rather than the reverse, so we wanted nothing of that. When Harry finally tracked down Urtain he said he couldn't speak English and the contract was in English. How could he sign? The

EBU official explained it all to him, but still he wouldn't sign. Finally they translated into Spanish and he signed. It was murder. Harry went greyer and greyer by the hour.

Harry Levene at that time was undoubtedly top dog in British boxing promotion. For years there had been two camps, those of Jack Solomons and Harry Levene. Fortunately for me, because Jim Wicks never tied me to one camp, we always played one against the other. When Solomons was in big time promoting we would drop a hint in the right quarters that Levene wanted us for so-and-so. Because both camps have their spies it was known the next day, and Solomons would be on the phone. Then we'd drop a hint for the Levene spies to pick up, and Harry would be on the phone to Jim. That was business. You got the most you could out of the situation. To have tied ourselves to one promoter or the other would have been fatal, but it's what some managers with young kids are doing now. Once it gets known that they are tied then the other promoters don't even try for them. So in some respects they are cutting their own throats, though it's difficult to break the system.

The biggest commercial promoter at the moment is Levene, because Jack Solomons has concentrated on the World Sporting Club. Just after the war Solomons was top Charlie. He was the first man to form a syndicate of interested parties, financial, managing and promoting, and he had everything his own way. He could get on to all the managers and say I want your boy to fight so-and-so, and I'll give him such-and-such. There was no one to challenge him; he had no rival. Levene has been the strongest for the last ten years. My first fight under Levene was against Zora Folley at Wembley in October 1958. Harry always swears that he uses his own money. He works closely with Jarvis Astaire, who looks after the closed circuit television aspect. Micky Duff is Harry's match-maker, though he always reckons to make the top-of-the-bill fight himself. A lot of managers feel they have got to stay the right side of Micky.

Solomons was gradually overtaken by Levene, and finally switched to promoting for the World Sporting Club, a private members' club with the main boxing matches going on after dinner. The boxers' purse comes out of the members' fees and television revenue. I could never box for a dinner show as there wasn't enough money in it. They could only pay £1,000 at the most, unless it was a TV night. If I was starting all over again it might be different, but certainly I don't care much for the idea. It's not that I would object to boxing in front of a lot of people wining and dining, but I was brought up on commercial shows from which you build a following. Most of my early fights were at Harringay Arena and even in that short time George and me found we had a following which stayed very loyal to us and encouraged others to support us. It was a good way to begin. When you fight in clubs you don't create a following. Ken Buchanan is a classic example. His first twenty or so fights were in clubs, and he never really built a following until he started to appear on TV. And that's not the same as a flesh and blood support. He never boxed in small shows. He's Scottish, a world champion in 1971, the best light-weight we have, but he's never boxed before a big crowd in Scotland, and not much more in England. So he's a draw in America but until recently he didn't sell tickets here. The mistake was to be on too many club shows. Jim Wicks would ensure that we would never have less than £6,000 worth of tickets to sell and give away for a big show. Sometimes it was up to £10,000. The promoter really wanted you if you did that. We'd have tickets for Jim's friends, my friends, family, and a whole lot of close supporters. Ken Buchanan, I read once, bought four ringside seats for one of his fights.

I like Harry Levene because you can talk to him man to man, but he's not easy to do business with. He's shrewd and hard, and he's been in the game a long time, nearly as long as Jim Wicks. Harry was the youngest manager of all time, looking after boxers when he was fifteen or sixteen years old. In boxing we've a bit of jargon, and to 'choke' means to get money out of someone. Well, Jim Wicks always said that Harry choked more promoters with 'dead bodies' (that is boxers who, to put it mildly, are not going to win a world championship) than any other manager. But he's a likeable fellow. He lived for years in Park Lane but a little while ago he moved to a penthouse near Marble Arch. He's a wealthy man, but if you are in his office and you want to make a phone call, even if it's only ten pence, and even if it's as much in his business interest as yours, he'll say, 'Put that in the petty cash, Henry.' Jim reckoned to get that back with a few hundred quid interest!

If you do a deal with Harry it's like the Houses of Parliament. Some promoters would have a bad house and then hum and hah, wanting you to take a bit less. You never got that with Harry. If it was an agreed sum you never got less and he'd pay you if the house was empty. Harry's the sort of fellow you exchange Christmas cards with—it doesn't matter that he's Jewish as far as that is concerned—and if you are fighting a foreigner he'll come in the dressing-room to wish you luck and genuinely want you to win. But in general we had a business relationship with him. Jim says he couldn't afford otherwise. If Harry has invited him out ninety-nine times, Jim reckons he's settled the bill ninety-eight. He's exaggerating, of course, but I think Harry would agree he doesn't exactly throw his money around.

That was why he was in a bit of a tizz when he offered all that cash to Urtain and the Spaniard started mucking him around. It was while I was in training for this fight that the scientific team from the RAF's Institute of Aviation Medicine analysed those 6,600 camera pictures taken in six seconds, and found that when I started to launch the left hook it travelled fifteen times faster than the Saturn Five rocket that takes astronauts to the moon. The force on landing approached three tons. It was fantastic. When I read it I wondered why I'd lost so many fights! Perhaps someone translating that accounted for Urtain and his strange carryings-on.

When eventually we got him into the ring I was at the weight I liked, 13 stone 7½, and I just kept pumping left hands into his face. His head bothered me a bit. He was shorter and slower than me and his head was always waving about under my eyes and chin.

In the first round I had a bit of a cut, but Eddie Thomas did his job well and I wasn't bothered again. Urtain was bodily a very strong fighter, and tough, but without technique. If they could have taught him how to set up a man for a punch, jab, jab and then the right, he would have been a far more dangerous fighter. But he just slung the right hand on a hit or miss basis. That may be OK when you are fighting mugs, but when you step up into world class you have to be able to set up punches. My lefts did a lot of damage. His eye swelled up, he had a cut and the referee stopped the fight at the end of the eighth round. I think if he'd have come out again I would have knocked him out. He caught me with one loopy punch to the body in the fifth, but it didn't make me groggy or shake me severely.

Between November 1970 and March 1971 my thoughts about retirement crystallised. It doesn't come suddenly. For two years I'd been thinking the time was getting near. It's little things that happen. Jim could see them too. We'd signed to defend against Joe Bugner on March 16, at Wembley, and I was staying at the Clive Hotel, Hampstead, and training in the Board's gym in Haverstock Hill. It's in the gym while you're working that you get your signals. Four or five years previously I would go through maybe five sparring partners in a two-week pre-fight build-up. I knew a couple of them wouldn't last because I would be knocking them out. But in the last eighteen months to a year that wasn't happening. The timing wasn't there quite like it used to be. Two sparring partners would last the fortnight. I would hurt them and perhaps knock them down, but at one time they would be so knocked out, even with the 16-ounce gloves, that they didn't want to know again. These are the important signals.

I have heard critics say that I was hard on sparring partners, but I never believed in pulling punches in the gym because if you did it there you would start doing it in the ring. We always paid sparring partners a lot of money—they would get £20 a round, some of them, which is more than they would get in a fight. So, naturally, they had to expect to work hard and I wouldn't expect them to pull punches. We had our big gloves and our headguards, after all. Two we used a lot—Joey Armstrong, a tough, compact, coloured fighter—and the American, Buddy Turman. We used Joey for five or six fights but after that he got less sharp and keen and I found I was stopping him. Then we got Buddy. He was a good fighter, too, and I'll always remember the first time I knocked him out in the gym with the big gloves. He just couldn't believe it. He sat in the dressing-room with his head in his hands. It did more damage to his morale than it ever did to his physical condition. There's a time early on in a good boxer's life when he doesn't think he's ever going to get stopped and it's a bit of a shock when he is. 'How did it happen? What did you do?' he was saying. 'I just hit you with a good left hook,' I said.

You can't switch off being the champion just because you're in the gym. That's the place which helps make you the champion.

It wasn't leaving a comfortable home that began to get me in training but my physical reactions when I started sparring. Sparring is what you are training to do. I found in the first two or three days that I was stiffening up. If I over-reached or pulled a muscle it would take me over a week to shake off the stiffness and soreness. The muscles weren't as supple as they used to be. When the Bugner fight was arranged Jim and I never said in so many words that it was going to be the last, but that was the understanding between us. About a fortnight before the fight I actually came out with it on the phone one evening to Albina. I told her Jim and I had had a chat and this was really going to be the last. She said, 'Thank God for that.'

Jim and I had finally got around to mentioning it, and Jim had said we could earn enough money publicity wise, opening this and sponsoring that. Albina was obviously much relieved, but I can't say I felt either relief or disappointment. It had all happened too gradually and inevitably. Plenty of people would have talked me out of the ring ten years before, but that was *them* telling *me*. This was our decision. And it was made not on the strength of a performance in the ring, which critics would use as a yardstick, but on our performance in the gym playing our practice shots. I was thirty-seven, and boxing is really a young man's sport. It was only hard training that kept me in good condition at that age.

In 1969 I could think of taking Ellis for a world championship fight, but although Joe Frazier was now champion there was never a chance of a last big pay day. Even if we had been offered him Jim would have turned it down. He'd have turned him down in 1966 or 1962, come to that. Boxing is a matter of styles. Jack Bodell had no earthly chance against Jerry Quarry when he fought him in 1971. If Quarry could have picked any opponent he couldn't have chosen better than a big fellow who comes rushing at him, leaves his chin hanging up in the air all exposed, and a southpaw. Quarry is a great right-hand counter-puncher, the perfect weapon against Bodell, and Jack was finished almost before he'd started. It would have happened with me and Frazier or me and Sonny Liston. Jim would never have agreed to the match because of the styles. Liston was a big man, over fifteen stone. He outweighed me by two stone. Jim always said he was too ugly, but that was his way of saying he didn't want to fight that type of guy. Liston was a fighter — he had a fair left jab and a good right hand, but he was in boxing terms an animal. And Jim, thank God, thought too much of me to let me in the same ring. With Ali we'd have gone in every day of the week. But not Liston, or Frazier. Both are sluggers, coming forward and hitting hard, giving you no rest, and two stone heavier. Some of the Germans were heavy maulers, but not in the same class. Ellis is a box-fighter, and Ali, too — a fancy Dan who couldn't really hurt you. I'm not saying Ali wasn't in the same class, but he was a different style. You could have a rest against him because you would be chasing him whereas the other two would be chasing you. They were slugger-killers from the hard American school. You could hit Frazier with your Sunday punch and you could break your hand. He'd shake his head and come on after you. Those guys can also break your heart.

Young Joe Bugner, on the face of it, was not a heart-breaker. I'd seen him on several occasions, sixteen years younger than myself, 15 stone $2\frac{1}{4}$ to my 13 stone 7. A strong guy, with a fair left hand, but I knew in my heart I could mess the kid about, which basically I think I did. My ambition was to retire as undefeated British, European and Commonwealth heavyweight champion. Bugner had a lot going for him. He was two or three inches taller, he was a stone and a half heavier and he'd had thirty-six professional fights. Clay and Patterson won the world heavyweight title with less. Bugner had the backing of a lot of top people in British boxing. Andy Smith was his manager but he was working very closely with Micky Duff and Jarvis Astaire.

These days, if you have a British boy with the skill, capa-bility, know-how and stamina to take on a big fight then a British promoter can compete with America where pre-viously he couldn't. When Ali came over here it was the biggest pay day he had until he fought Frazier at Madison Square Garden on March 8, 1971, with a million pounds guaranteed the boxers. Over here he got something like £100,000 without taking into account the ancillary rights from America. With closed circuit television, most big cities can see the fight on the night. Usually there is a filmed build-up to the big fight with one or two supporting contests, then boxing personalities and critics discuss the prospects. I've been on several of these since my retirement and it creates a good atmosphere. There's also a tidy income with people in the cinemas paying £2 to £5 a ticket.

I was lucky in that all these 'extras' were available in the latter part of my boxing career. There is no doubt that I was the top paid British boxer of all time. My fight with Ali went all over Europe, the Far East, Australia and America. But the first TV satellite only went to a certain height and when it disappeared over the horizon you'd had it. The latest one can beam a fight anywhere and there's no waiting. So you've the world as a potential audience where before it was limited. It was possible therefore for Bugner to be on the verge of a £250,000 pay-out, over two or three years, if he beat me. But he had to prove he was a draw, that people wanted to see him and were prepared to support him. There was a lot on this fight for him and his connections.

There was a 10,000 crowd at Wembley that night, March 16, 1971, and plenty of atmosphere. It was the old against the new, with the new boy still to capture the fans. The first round was more or less as we predicted; we knew Joe had a good left and that he would jab out hoping to start trouble around my left eye. I didn't want to rush—that's not my style—but to keep the pressure on. Joe isn't as good a fighter going backwards as he is coming forwards. The early rounds in fact were a bit of a see-saw. I won one, he won one and up to ten rounds nothing separated us. In the corner after the tenth Jim said, 'Look, you've got to do something. You're letting this guy get on top too much.' So after that I had a spurt and I reckon I won the 11th, 12th, 13th and 14th. He had a good last round, but being a little generous, and giving him that, I thought I had won by three-quarters of a point. He was more tired than me in the 13th and 14th rounds, and I thought they clinched it. All the good judges read the fight as I did. Before the 15th, Jim said, 'You've only got to stay on your feet and you've got it.'

As the final bell went I moved towards the referee, Harry Gibbs, of London, to give him my hand. This is something you learn in boxing. If you're pretty sure you've won you don't give the referee time to dally. You know he's checked his card right up to the last round, and he's going to make it a quick decision. So I went up to him. But he ignored my hand and turned his back on me. I thought, 'Cor, stone me.' Then he went over to Bugner and it sunk in that I wasn't getting the verdict. All hell was suddenly let loose. They had to get the police up to escort Gibbs out of the ring. Peter Wilson wrote in the *Daily Mirror*, 'The crowd booed and snarled like an angry animal with ten thousand heads.' By my reckoning I had won nine of the fifteen rounds, but Harry Gibbs had me losing by a quarter of a point.

I've been boxing long enough and I think I am my own best judge. I reckon I know if I have won or lost. The clearest thing I remember is the disbelief on the faces in Bugner's corner as Harry Gibbs went over to them. They were more surprised in their corner than we were disappointed in ours. In this game you learn to control yourself. But that night it was a good job George, my brother, kept hold of Jim or he would have been over there to stick one on Harry Gibbs's chin. I've never seen him so upset before or since.

When you have given your best in a fight and you've done enough to win and they go and give it to the other guy, you feel completely deflated and choked up. No one could have been more upset than me, but what could you do? All the protesting in the world was not going to help. Unless the referee had made a mistake counting his card there was nothing to be done. Ranting and raving can't alter a verdict at that stage. There were one or two people who came into the dressing-room to commiserate afterwards who we knew were up in the air with joy. Some people had a lot of money on Bugner to win the fight, and although they said how sorry they were we knew blooming well it was lip service. But I don't want to start knocking the sport at the last. Boxing has been good to me and I don't want ill feelings. I'm not interested in betting and have never bet on a fight in my life. For one thing I don't understand it! People would come up to me and say, 'You're six to one on.' And I'd say, 'Yeah. Yeah,' but I wouldn't know whether I was or not. I don't think boxing in Britain has a crooked side so far as fighting is concerned. You could say, I suppose, that I wasn't approached because I was unapproachable, but I couldn't give the name of one person who had fixed a fight in seventeen years of boxing.

Fixing a fight is not an easy thing to do. No top heavyweight would take ten grand to go crooked. What is ten grand if he knows he can earn more by fighting straight and losing? And if he wins, if he has the luck, he could be on to a million dollar purse. It's laughable to suggest that a fight would be thrown for ten grand. Who in Britain has ten grand to offer in any case? Liston is supposed to have stunk the place out when he was knocked out in the first round by Clay in their second world title fight at Lewiston, Maine, in May 1965. It may be that he went in not to fight, but no one will ever convince me that he took money to lose it. Liston always looked good against a fighter who wanted to come in and have a slug. But smart guys who could move and jab could make him look silly. And he simply realised that Clay was one of those guys. In the first fight I think he went in believing he could stop Clay in three or four rounds even with arm trouble. But when he found he couldn't handle Clay he obviously said to himself, 'What have I chewed off here?' Every fighter has a bogyman and Clay was his. Liston was slinging punches in the air, and if you've pulled an arm muscle that's the worst thing you can do. It only aggravates the trouble. In the second fight I think he just said to himself he didn't want to know this guy. He knew he couldn't handle him. It goes back to styles and the way some boxers can psych others. I've never really thought in my heart of hearts that Ali had a punch in the heavyweight division. I'm sure he's won so many fights inside the distance and looked as though he has knocked them out because he's half beaten these men before they have gone into the ring. It happens with the coloured boys more often because they are more gullible or susceptible. It's not a lack of concentration so much as their upbringing and way of life. They're more flamboyant and they tend to take things at their face value more readily. They're either on top of the world or they're down. We delve into things a bit more and don't believe so easily. Ali believed in himself and his new religion, and it made him that much more formidable. Some fighters have gone in against him pretty well on their knees—Zora Folley was one—almost asking to be knocked out. Several were past their best and looking for a good pay day quick, and I'm not discounting the Black Muslim movement, which was a powerful force. The coloured guy can't easily buck them. Ali represented the black movement at a point where it was very close to rebellion, so when he was in the ring in Atlanta or even New York he had this vast army of Negro supporters. That was worth a lot to him.

CHAPTER TWENTY-TWO

Life in and out of a boxing ring teaches a certain philosophy and knowledge of human nature. You learn a lot about yourself. I'm not, I think, particularly aggressive with my views, although I've earned a living from physical aggression. No one has ever seriously picked on me outside the ring, not in the way Tommy Farr used to get it in his pub, anyway. I'm very easy going. People can insult me but I can just let things go by. Sometimes in conversation you may make a remark and a guy will jump on you, contradicting and snapping, and you can tell he's wanting an argument and perhaps a fight. You can tell that straightaway. So I look at him and say, well, you're entitled to your opinion, and I'm entitled to mine, and just let it go at that. Over the years in boxing you learn to control yourself. When I'm driving someone can cut me up and I say, 'You sloppy so-and-so', but a lot of people would want to jump out and start swearing and shouting, getting something out of their own systems perhaps. I never really feel like that. Someone would have to do something really diabolical to make me lose my temper. I suppose I got rid of it all in the ring, and in training. I can watch a boxing match quite dispassionately—I don't get excited at all. Self-control is pumped into you over the years. If you get excited during a fight and do your nut then you are in worse trouble. So in the end it becomes second nature to control your feelings. I get more excited watching football than I ever do boxing. I'll jump and shout over athletics, too. I shall never forget Lillian Board coming from behind in one of her races and beating the field. I stood up and shouted myself hoarse. It was the same when England won the World Cup final in 1966. But for boxing I couldn't get that excited. I could see Jack

Johnson knock out Jack Dempsey and I wouldn't open my mouth except to comment on the technique of it. Yet I love boxing, I really love to see it still. But it's in the head, not an emotional thing, as if I'm in the ring doing it to the other fellow, and I've got to keep calm.

It's a matter of professionalism, and what it teaches you. Jackie Stewart, the motor racing driver, said once that his first thought when there was a crash in front of him during a race was how to get round it and get in front. Only after that would he look in his mirror and think, gosh, that looks bad, hope he's OK. That's how I felt in a fight. Your first instinct is self-preservation and all champions must have it. You are there to win at all costs. It's the killer instinct. If I saw a man with a cut eye I didn't think, 'Oh dear, what a terrible eye.' I said, 'Good! Wallop! Take that! Take that!' I wanted to play on it. I knew if that eye got bad enough the referee was going to stop the fight. If you're feeling sorry for the guy you won't get to the top. Ali never stood back and said, 'Oh, look at Henry's poor eye.' He knew I couldn't see the punches coming and he threw plenty. I don't feel ashamed of my feelings, and I wouldn't expect Ali to feel ashamed for himself. How can I feel ashamed for working on a cut eye when it has happened to me in reverse dozens of times? We've chosen a tough business—and I'm talking here only of feelings and attitudes in the ring. Outside, it is totally different. Once you accept that given half a chance an opponent is going to work on your eye, and vice versa, then you begin to get on. When I had the spell of four defeats in 1956 and 1957 I wasn't looking at it like that. Up to then I was worried about myself, whether I was going to hurt my eye. The turning point was when I forgot about mine and made the other fellow worry about his.

The M1 can be a more dangerous place than a boxing ring or a racing track, because there are people on it who don't know what they are doing. If you know an opponent's experience you can anticipate what he is capable of doing. You can't anticipate a mug. In the amateur days I'd sooner have fought Madigan than someone I knew nothing about. When I was in the Army I could come up against a rank novice in the unit or battalion championships. Those guys bring you down to their level because they are doing unorthodox things. If you are fighting an experienced boxer you can anticipate roughly what he is going to do. But with the mugs, you think they are going to go one way, for example to get out of a tight spot in a corner, or to get off the ropes, but instead they go the other, which in theory puts them in worse trouble. You think he is out of distance and he slings a big, swingy punch which possibly catches you. I would as soon be in the ring with an ABA champion.

A boxer's life is devoted to physical fitness. Yet, like everyone else, you don't give a lot of thought to it until you are ill. When you are unwell you suddenly realise how miserable you are and what you are missing. If I see a big fat guy, I don't think, 'Cor, look at him, the big slob. I'm glad I'm fit and not like him.' Naturally there are moments when you are more conscious of your fitness. It's lovely to wake up in the morning and feel good after your four-mile run. And days in the gym when I've knocked down one or two of my sparring parners, or knocked hell out of the bag, I've thought, 'Good, I'm coming to my peak.' But these are only little moments of satisfaction. In boxing training the fitter you are the harder you push yourself, so it never really comes easy. I always trained to go fifteen rounds so there was never a time when I hated myself for being unfit or short of basic condition for a professional fight. It never happened. Nor did I ever take a serious beating in my career. The only times I might be short of 100 per cent fitness would be fighting exhibitions. After a few rounds you're puffing and blowing like a good 'un, and you think, 'Cor blimey, I'm out of condition. If I'd done a little bit of training I'd be a lot better.'

That was not the reason, though, for me refusing an exhibition with Ali when he visited Britain in 1971. That was a matter of pride. I have always employed sparring partners during training, but I am no one's sparring partner. That's the difference. When you have been a champion you don't become anyone's sparring partner and I don't care who it is that asks you—a triple world champion for all I care. If they had said go in with Ali and have three rounds, I'd have gone in—as long as I got the same money. But I'm not going in knowing that Ali is getting 22,000 dollars and I'm going to end up with 3,000. Knowing Ali, he would want to stick one in just to show he was the boss. I would come back at him and it would develop into a ding-dong. I can have fights for nothing anywhere.

I have mentioned my ability to relax before a big fight. I think I was lucky in being born the way I was, without a nervous disposition. But I think the game and its demands can help teach you further relaxation. Nerves never got on top of me, and that's as well, because nerves are more weakening than actual physical pressure or damage. There have been a lot of good fighters in the past who never became great because of a mental approach. They reckon if Eddie Phillips could have got Joe Louis in the gym and no one had told him it was Louis he'd have knocked him out. But on the big occasions he couldn't reproduce the form in the ring. Phillips fought once for the British title, against Len Harvey in December 1938, and he was disqualified in the fourth round. But once I finished my training the day before a fight I could go back to my hotel and sit there for two hours literally thinking of nothing, my mind a complete blank. The Beatles went halfway across the world trying to learn relaxation, but I could do it for nothing, thank goodness.

Outside the ring I had the advantage all my life of being a big fellow, so that no one ever seemed to want to pick a fight. The one occasion someone tried I shall never forget. It was on our twenty-sixth birthday and Jim Wicks had taken George and me out to lunch. So I'm driving Jim Back home to Eltham on a windy sort of day when I overtake a cyclist. I might have pulled in a little bit sharpish—about twenty-five yards ahead, I suppose, which wasn't quite enough room. His head was down against the wind and rain and it was a little bit downhill. Anyway, a moment or two after I pulled up I heard a slight thud. Out of the corner of my eye I saw a bike being pushed alongside the car, and I rolled down the window—a silly thing to do on these occasions! Before I could say anything, bosh!—a back-hander has come right through the open window. Jim jumps out, George jumps out, I jump out—two six-foot, 14-stone, fit-as-a-fiddle boxers, and Jim's no midget. There's this fellow, as thin as my little finger, five-foot nothing and about fifty. We all said, 'You cheeky so-and-so.' He looks us up and down and says, 'Yeah, you feel brave, don't you, just cos there's three of you!' And I really believe if there had just been one of us he'd have had a go! Anyway, that broke the tension and we three started laughing. He didn't see the funny side, mark you. He just got on his bike and pedalled off muttering. I was left with a fat lip, but I still had to laugh.

One of the biggest decisions of my life was to have Jim Wicks manage my affairs. Often people have inquired how much it was me, and how much Jim, when we protested, for example, when we gave up the British heavyweight title after ten years, when we tried to get the need for a tax-spreadover raised in the House of Commons and when we had our tussles with the Boxing Board of Control and the European Boxing Union. I paid a manager to arrange fights, get the best terms he could, do the business connected with it and do the protesting if he thought it necessary. If he's a good manager he knows what to do and what not to do. Jim certainly knew the boxing game. But he always said that on most occasions it wasn't the manager's basic job to protest. All fights have a steward in charge and he should be the man to protest to the British Boxing Board of Control. But too often he doesn't, and when he doesn't it is the manager who has to decide whether to open his mouth or not. The trouble is that if a manager keeps on protesting the Board start to dislike him and he gets a reputation for being a moaner. Some of the outstanding incidents of my career could have been settled by the stewards. There was the occasion when they came up with only half the correct amount of bandages in my fight with Brian London at Belle Vue. Jim shouldn't really have needed to make such a stand, and threaten that we wouldn't leave the dressing-room. There is no doubt in our minds that something should have been done over what went on in Clay's corner between rounds after I knocked him down in the first fight. It wasn't any good protesting afterwards. Nothing could change the verdict. But something might have been done at the time.

Another incident that sticks in my mind involved not myself but Terry Downes, when he fought Paul Pender for the American's world middleweight title in London in July 1961. The fight was held up for half an hour or more because Pender had so much bandage on his hands. The Board ordered him to take it off and he refused. 'If you don't allow it I'm not going to fight,' he said, and they gave way. They wouldn't have given way if Downes had had a mile of bandage on. They'd have said, 'Take it off or you're suspended.' But they didn't even fine Pender.

Boxers have to believe in themselves. In the ring part of their game is to deceive, by feinting and dodging, but it is self-deception of the worst kind to fight knowing deep down that not enough training has been done. A fighter who has kidded himself in that way will rarely come off against a determined, fit opponent. On the other hand I've been hit on the chin and gone down on the floor knowing, before I've got up even, that I've got the beating of the other fellow. My fight against Dick Richardson at Porthcawl in September 1958 was a classic example. Dick shook me but I wasn't really groggy. I knew he would come in after me and leave himself open, which is what he did. That sort of conviction comes from belief in yourself and that your training has been right. There was never a fight where I pushed myself to the verge of exhaustion. If you've done that then your training is wrong. I can remember only one major fight where a boxer collapsed from exhaustion. That was Jack Gardner against Johnny Williams, where Williams collapsed afterwards. I'm sure that affected Williams psychologically for years after.

Mental strain takes a lot of forms. You can knock a man out in one round and still feel as tired at midnight as if you'd gone the full fifteen rounds. The excitement of the whole affair is causing you to burn up as much nervous energy as physical. It's the same if you are travelling anywhere special. You are tired at the finish because you have burned up energy with the excitement. I can't say I ever felt over-tired. I would drive myself home and we would unwind with a few drinks. Albina and I would chat away about almost anything except the fight. I wouldn't have slept well if I had gone straight to bed. In fact it always took a night or two after a big fight before I could go off like a log. But then I would, from nine in the evening to nine in the morning.

I am not, I suppose, an over-imaginative man. I have to think hard to remember a time when I was really afraid, and that was back in the war on a particular night when the doodlebugs were coming over thick and fast. We spent the whole night in the shelter, and the guns never stopped. In the early morning when we came out they were still banging away. George and me looked at each other and I said, 'Do you think we're being invaded?' It must have been 1944, so looking back there wasn't so much prospect of an invasion, but we were only ten and we were suddenly really scared. We felt kind of hopeless and helpless. We couldn't do anything about it. But that soon passed. As kids you never worried about anything for very long. The one other time when I was really scared, and it was in the ring, was when Joe Erskine fell over the bottom rope on his back. I really thought he had broken his spine or something, and so did Jim. We were both relieved and happy when they revived him. Otherwise I have been very lucky. We never felt threatened or repressed as children, although we were a relatively poor family. There was always a hope, and it was up to us to get out and do.

CHAPTER TWENTY-THREE

Everyone needs just a bit of luck on the way to the top, although I do believe that you largely make your own luck. Boxers are very superstitious people. I always boxed in the same colours, royal blue and white, and I never changed them. For each fight the Lonsdale sports equipment people presented me with a new pair of shorts. I had a dressing-gown of royal blue velvet with a Union Jack made for the world heavyweight title fight and I never wore anything else afterwards. It was a beautiful thing, all hand embroidered, and again given by Lonsdale. Another crazy thing was that I never cleaned my boxing boots. I never put polish on them. That was taboo—unlucky. I always put in new laces, but I never polished them because once in my amateur days I did it before a fight with Erskine. The army team I fought for that night was dead favourite to win and I was the only fighter who lost.

Boxing boots would last quite a few years, even without polish, but you would always reckon to break them in while training. You would never wear them new in the ring. On the night of a fight I wore ordinary white nylon football socks. They were on the long side but I would roll them down to make them look neat. I always taped my laces, as I've explained, though a lot just let them dangle. There's nothing worse than to have to stop and tie up a lace.

Other boxers' superstitions can be more curious or sentimental still. Willie Pastrano, the American light-heavyweight world champion, always laced his wedding ring on to the lace of his left boot. Some fighters always put the same boot on first. Some would have an old dressing-gown which might be so tatty it barely covered them, but they reckoned it was lucky so they kept it. George Chuvalo, the Canadian heavyweight, always changed in his dressing-room wearing his trilby hat. He never took the hat off until he was due to go into the ring. You could see him walking round nude in the dressing-room, but always with his hat on. An amateur boxer we knew always kept his ginger wig on until he got into the corner. When the bell went he would whip off his wig and there he was, totally bald, like Yul Brynner. Terrified some of his opponents, he did. I reckon that's how he won most of his fights.

Cars have been one of my passions outside boxing, and I suppose have reflected my career. George and I bought our first, an old square Ford Prefect, just after our first professional fight. It was an old black second-hand job but it was a good little runner. And it was in that car that we had the sort of accident which a foot one way or the other would have finished one or both of the Cooper twins. We were on our way home from a fight with Joe Erskine in the Harringay Arena on November 15, 1955. Bern and his wife, Cory, who was about six months' pregnant, were in the car with us. Going down Balls Pond Road there was suddenly a great thump at a crossroads, and our Prefect spun round and rolled over twice. When we found where the doors were we climbed out. I was more concerned for Cory than anything, but the guy who had hit us—he was driving a big Wolseley—came over all concerned for me. I was covered in cuts and bruises, not from the crash but from Joe Erskine's fists. I'd lost the fight and it showed! 'Cor, I never expected to see anyone get out of there alive,' he said. The car was near enough diamond-shaped from the collision and virtually a write-off.

After that I came up in the world and bought a new Morris Cowley, then a Fiat 1800, then a Mark II Jaguar. It was a 2·4 and a bit underpowered so I got a Mark X, but that was a bit big and banana-shaped, so I went back to a smaller, sportier car, the Alfa-Romeo T1. Then Alfa brought out a sportier model still, the GT, and I had a go at that. Then it was a Mercedes 220 SE coupé, and after that a Bentley T series, near enough seven grand's worth of motor car. I got very ostentatious with that one! I was earning big money and I thought I'd treat myself before I gave it all to the tax man. I had little bits of trouble with it and after fourteen months I got rid of it for nearly what I'd paid, which was the best thing about it. After that came the best car I ever had, the Jensen Interceptor, and I kept it the longest, too—three years. I really enjoyed it, and I only sold it because the boys were getting bigger and it wasn't very comfortable in the back for them. After that I got a 280 SE Mercedes saloon, and then a BMW 30 S, a three-litre saloon with plenty of room but with a sports car performance. I've a weakness for fast cars. I never smoked, I never drank much, I never went to night clubs, but I enjoy a good car. I only know the most elementary things about them and I hate having to open the bonnet and fiddle around. We go to the Continent every year and I like a car that can cruise at 100 mph on those roads. If you're doing four or five hundred miles a day you don't want to be chugging round at 70.

I've said that I think the M1 can be more dangerous than the boxing ring and unfortunately within a fortnight of buying the BMW there were the marks to prove it. Coming back from Birmingham late one night I'm driving along, the last of a line of three cars. There was patchy fog and we drove through it carefully—it was mist rather than fog. We'd just started picking up a bit of speed when another patch closed in. Instead of slowing, the guy in front suddenly jammed on his brakes as hard as he could. The back of his car lifted right up on its springs. I pulled out to the side to miss him, but once my offside wheels got into the mud in the centre it was just as if my brakes were locked one side. It just dragged me up to the centre barrier and though

I didn't even dent that it certainly dented my BMW, all down one side, about £150 worth. The car in front went merrily on its way and the driver never knew what happened.

I still like boxing. I like to watch it and I enjoy the atmosphere. In a few years' time it would be nice to get hold of a young heavyweight prospect and coach and manage him. I feel that I know what it takes to be a heavyweight more than, say, a flyweight. I've no ambition, I'm afraid, to go into boys' club boxing. It's a rotten thing to say, but I just wouldn't have the patience to have thirty kids in a club running round like we did. Men like Georgie Page who train these boys are a special breed indeed. What I'd like to do and what I will do are probably two different things, because it's getting harder all the time to find young men who want to be professional fighters and are prepared to dedicate themselves to make the grade. The rewards are much higher now, but we've a welfare state and there aren't the really hungry people around, people fighting and striving to better themselves. There were 3,000 to 4,000 professional boxers before the war. Now there are scarcely 300. Boxing thrives on hard times, and life now is too comfortable: if there's any danger with an activity then you mustn't take part in it. There are all these people who want to ban boxing, and we are becoming a nation of watchers and not doers. Men weren't built to be cabbages. An element of danger, and the need to beat it, is a driving force in men's lives.

Baroness Summerskill thinks boxing is a dangerous sport. Well, fair enough, she is entitled to her views and I respect her for sticking to what she believes, but she is not entitled to force them on to other people any more than I am entitled to force my views on her. After my retirement I went to a discussion on boxing on Yorkshire TV, remembering a similar programme when Jack Solomons and one or two other boxing people got heated with Baroness Summerskill. She's a great debater, she's been in the House of Commons, she's in the House of Lords now, and talking is her business. She tied them up and made them all a bit sick. So I thought, well, I'll not go there and be aggressive, I'll listen to what she has to say, and I'll agree with some of it because I *do* agree. But not with everything. I think my attitude may have surprised her a bit, and perhaps she felt she ought to try to shake me. Suddenly she looked straight at me and said, 'Mr Cooper, have you looked in the mirror lately and seen the state of your nose?' I thought, 'Blimey, here's me being a goodie goodie, and that's all I get for it!' I couldn't help it, she'd left herself wide open. So I came straight back, 'Well, Madam, have you looked in the mirror and seen the state of your nose lately? Boxing is my excuse. What's yours?' The audience roared. I think we came out winning on points.

CHAPTER TWENTY-FOUR

Over the years you hear of so many fighters going broke that you wonder how you will cope when your time comes to retire. Although I had been the highest paid British fighter ever, you can't accumulate wealth in this country, at least not as a boxer is taxed, and that creates a nagging worry. When I retired I couldn't sit back and think, 'I don't have to do anything for the rest of my life.' If I could have done a deal with the Inland Revenue so that they took as much as half my money then I might have been able to relax. But if I'd earned £250,000 I hadn't kept more than £60,000. The year of the world title fight brought me in £50,000, but in hard cash it was worth only £7,000 to £8,000. All the same I had a tidy little sum to invest. I don't play the Stock Exchange, but I have a small amount invested. Charles St George, a friend I met through Jim and Harry Levene, is an insurance broker, and I have become a director of two of his companies. I don't know a great deal about insurance at this moment, but as the years go by I think I shall get more involved, probably on the public relations side. I am in a Lloyd's underwriting syndicate, too. Lloyd's is made up of syndicates—people who put up, say, £10,000 and underwrite the risk on whatever is insured. If it's an oil tanker your syndicate may decide to take a share in the risk. If anything goes wrong you stand to lose a proportion of your ten grand. But if all goes right you get a share of the profit. I'm on marine, so if there's anything colliding in the Channel I'm on the phone quick as lightning, 'Charles, did we have anything to do with that?' Lloyd's has been going through a sticky time the last few years, but in 1971–2 they made quite a profit, and the prospects are good.

There are plenty of people with ideas for spending my money. Some people approached me with an idea for hamburger machines from which we would make £20,000 a year. It was all worked out so lovely except where they would get the capital to buy the machines. I said, 'If it's as good as all that why don't you go to the bank for your loan?' My money was hard earned, and if there's any money to be played with I prefer that it's other people's. Jim still handles public appearances and the other PR work. We're on the phone every day and we still meet three times a week at our old haunts. I get more requests now than I did when I was boxing, mainly because people know I have more time. I've done three series as captain of one of the teams in the BBC's television quiz, *A Question of Sport*, but Wandsworth Borough Council really had me branching out when they got me to compere old-time music hall in Battersea Town Hall. I've not appointed a script writer yet, and if ever I'm short of a story I ring up my cousin, Bill Button, who's a character and a half. He's a driver and picks up a load of stories from the factories and firms he visits. Good, basic, earthy stuff!

I do as much as I can for two special charities—the club for kids with muscular dystrophy which dear old Freddie Mills started. When he died they more or less adopted me. I also got to know Lillian Board well. She lived at Ealing, not far from Wembley, and we were often asked to local functions together. Her death was a particular shock to Albina and me. We've associated ourselves closely with the Countess of Roxburgh's cancer appeal in Lillian's name.

All the activity seems to be keeping me fit enough. I haven't suddenly gone to seed after all those years of training. Four rounds of golf a week at my local club, Ealing, helps. If I can't get a round in I go over to the field at the back of the house for a bit of practice. I hit a ball every day if I can. I weighed myself after a year out of boxing and found I was 14 stone 6, which is only a stone over my best fighting weight. It was always my weight when I was out of serious training so I don't appear to have too much to worry about yet. Directly I start to feel sluggish I shall be straight off to the gym again. Golf may seem a big contrast, but it's competitive and I have to work at it to be efficient. It's a good mental exercise — you have to master your own frustration and aggravation. It gave me a bit of hope when I went down to John Jacobs's golf range with Graham Hill, the motor racing driver. After watching us for an hour, John, who's reckoned to be the top teaching professional in Britain, said he couldn't see why I shouldn't get my 19 handicap down to eight or nine within two years.

I have other ambitions. I'd love to have been to America. I just stopped over in Miami once, but I've never been to see places like Madison Square Garden, Jack Dempsey's restaurant and the famous gymnasiums. I'd like both my boys to take up amateur boxing, but I wouldn't force it on them. Henry is mad keen on soccer, and he has an interest in golf which I'm going to encourage. He likes to pull my trolley for me when I just want half-a-dozen holes at the golf club, and he's starting himself to give the ball a fair clip in the field at the back of our house. If he is good enough at the game it's a marvellous way to earn a living. But I am pleased, most of all, that I've an entry into Lloyd's and the insurance world, that he's going to a good school, and that when both boys leave school I can help them if they wish. It's nice to feel I've been able to create a secure future for my family.

While I like to work hard to achieve a particular goal I don't think I ever become a slave to things, not so that the enjoyment of life disappears, anyway. That certainly applies to my 'retirement'. I've a nice balance between doing things and relaxing. On a broadcast programme recently I looked at a week in my life. It began on the Monday with a BBC car collecting me at 9 am to be in the studio for Pete Murray's record programme by 9.30. I've known Pete for years, but I hadn't been on his programme for some time. He hands me record request cards and I read them out, he asks me questions about my career and I tell a few stories. The one about the old boy on the bike who gave me a biff always goes down well. Then he asks me about the state of boxing, and while I don't want to be too depressing about it I say I can't see many youngsters coming up. John Conteh, I say, could be a good prospect providing he fills out a bit. He's still only 13 stone 2 with a big meal inside him and his winter socks on. Cliff Morgan, the ex-Wales and British Lions rugby player who does a lot of commentary work for the BBC, is ill in a German hospital and just in case he is listening I send him a get-well message. At 1.15 I meet Jim Wicks at Simpson's and he tells me another supermarket wants me for the opening.

On Tuesday I am at Heathrow for the midday plane to Newcastle. Costain's have built a new town called Killingworth on the outskirts and have invited me to open it. The plane is delayed ninety minutes, but I get there in time for the civic dinner at the Gosforth Hotel. I chat with the mayor, the chief of police and the other civic heads, and the following day we go out to Killingworth for the ceremony and lunch. I'm back at home at Wembley at 8.30 in the evening. On the Thursday I have a golf lesson at 9 am, then play in a four-ball at Ealing.

On Friday I meet Jim at Sheekey's, as usual, at 12.30, and Frank Butler of *The News of the World* joins us for lunch. He's doing an article on young boxing prospects and wants my views. Afterwards I meet Albina, who has been shopping, and we pop in the Mazzini Garibaldi, a little club in Clerkenwell. It's an Italian social club, and apart from the golf club it's the only club I belong to. They're all very friendly and Albina can chatter away in Italian. Saturday afternoon I open a fete at Wembley, quite near home, then in the evening it's a charity ball at the Savoy. On the Sunday I've a TV recording for *A Question of Sport* in Manchester. That goes on every fortnight through the summer. I don't pick my own teams, the programme producers do that. With Cliff Morgan ill, Bobby Moore, the England soccer captain, is my rival captain on the programme. If I say it myself, I'm not too bad at the game. Monday comes round again and it's another recording in my home, but this time it's made by a chap from the London Electricity Board who has two mates in the Queen Victoria Hospital, East Grinstead, having plastic surgery to their faces. A generator blew up in front of them. I do a ten-minute tape with a few boxing and other stories to cheer them up. One of them, Danny Head, was a member of Bellingham Amateur Boxing Club, so I tell a few tales of the old times on Bellingham.

So I'm not exactly out at grass yet. I'm a member of all sorts of organisations, in some cases honorary where they just want my name on the old letterhead. I'm a member of the Vaudeville Golfing Society, and enough other golfing societies to play with a different one every day for a month if I had the time. I'm a Lord's Taverner, an association of cricket fans, many in television and show business. The Taverners raise money to help provide facilities for cricketers through the National Playing Fields Association. Prince Philip is our Patron and 'Twelfth Man' and in 1971-2 alone we raised £40,000. Albina has a better time of it now than when I was boxing. So many of the functions I went to then were stag—strictly men only. Now a lot more invitations are for the two of us.

We love a good party. Every year the Mazzini club has what we call a scampagnata, a midsummer's picnic for about a thousand of London's Italian community. It really is a great day, particularly if the weather is nice. We go independently by car to places like Woburn Abbey, the New Forest or Virginia Water. Most people make up parties and we're about twenty strong usually, with Albina's brothers and sisters and their families. After Mass in a giant marquee we'll set up our picnic tables, get out the salami, the pol-pettine, those lovely savoury meat balls, crispy bread, the old Chianti and Valpolicella bottles, and all the bits for a really good Italian nosh-up. Then, after siesta they start up the games—egg-and-spoon races, sack races, over-50 races, all that sort of thing. The men have a football match, the kids have their races, and then we finish up with dancing and singing in the marquee to a little accordion band. We sing all the Neapolitan songs—it's not exactly Gigli or La Scala but we have a lot of fun. Henry Marco and John Pietro love it of course. Henry's always wandering off. At home we're constantly having to ring round and fish him out of neighbours' houses. John's a lot quieter and doesn't like to stray far from me or his mother.

When we need a baby-sitter, Kathie Sweeney, who helps around the house during the week, is usually available. She's been with us for six years and of course to the boys is Auntie Kathie. Sometimes she is good enough to do it for the whole weekend if, for example, we have both been invited to a charity golf pro-am or something of the kind. It doesn't leave much time for the gardening, thank goodness. That's one thing I really hate. The only sort of gardening I reckon to do is on the golf course when I'm digging up divots. I had the front garden crazy-paved, with just a few beds here and there, to reduce the work a bit. Then we have a small lawn at the back. Albina is never short of flowers for the house in the summer, but for that we can thank our gardener, Paddy, who used to work in my shop. Paddy's a grafter, in his late fifties but strong as an ox. Somehow he keeps a bit of colour going all the year round, though how he does it I don't know. The other day he wanted a fiver for 150 gladioli. 'Where are you going to put them all?' I asked. It beats me how he does it when I've left so little of the garden unpaved.

I don't employ a secretary, though Charles St George has an office and two secretaries available and I shall probably be using them more as my insurance work grows. At home I answer letters with my own two-fingered typing, and that can take an hour or two each day. I get more letters now than at my peak as a fighter. Half the people I meet don't seem to realise I've retired. 'When are you going to fight Clay again?' they want to know. Fan letters still keep coming, new ones and old, maybe half-a-dozen each post. Every year I order 5,000 picture postcards of myself, and send them personally signed, usually with a little message, to fans. At something like the Killingworth new town opening I would take at least a hundred to hand round. I have to work at least four months ahead on my diary, especially for the opening of fetes and bazaars on a Saturday.

We love old friendships and family reunions. Mum and Dad enjoy pottering round the garden of their bungalow just outside Margate. It's a biggish garden and keeps them well occupied. But at Christmas and Easter they come up to spend a day or so with us, perhaps Christmas Day at my place and Boxing Day at George's or Bern's.

Jim is near enough eighty and takes things quietly now, though you don't mention this to his bookmaker. Jim has given him a right roasting for the last year or two. In any case Jim reckons my new career in public relations keeps him busier than when I was boxing—or that's what he tells everyone. Dear old Jim. His wife died about fifteen years ago, but he still lives in the same little house in Footscray

Road, Eltham, and so far as the Coopers are concerned he is as much a part of the family as ever. Not long ago he fell down badly and they took him off to hospital with a cut eye, among other things. 'Don't you touch that eye till the boy's here!' he told them. He reckons the boy—that's me—is a better expert on cuts than a doctor!

Bern and Cory lived off the Bromley Road in Catford until about fifteen years ago, when they moved to Guildford Grove, Greenwich, where they are still living. He's doing well as a heating engineer, though he won't start his own business because he says there is too much fuss and trouble with it. They have three children, Mark, Lynn and Neil.

George is at Farningham in Kent, on the A20 near Brands Hatch. They often joke because they are at the foot of Death Hill, re-named to draw attention to the danger there. He and Barbara have three young children, Darrell, Beth, and Gavin who was born in June 1972. George's plastering contractor's business specialises in artex, the decorative plastic finish which gives you stipples, swirls, fans and that sort of thing. He's doing very well. We reckon to visit each other at least once a fortnight.

Mum and Dad were up here last at Easter. Dad was telling his stories as usual. Mum sits back and doesn't say too much. But an interviewer calls one day and wants her to talk about me. She folds her hands together, and looks very prim and straight at him. 'Everything Henry's done he's done with his own two hands,' she says. I butt in : 'Yeah, but mostly with the left, mother.'

HENRY COOPER

Professional Record, 1954–1971

dis—disqualified; *dr*—draw; *ko*—knock out; *l*—lost; *pts*—points; *r*—round; *rsf*—referee stopped fight; *rtd*—retired; *w*—won.

> Number of fights 55
> Won 40
> Drew 1
> Lost 14

Wins		*Losses*	
Inside distance	27	Inside distance	8
Points	11	Points	5
Disqualifications	2	Disqualifications	1

1954
Sept 14   Harry Painter   *w ko*   *r*1   Harringay, London
Oct 19   Dinny Powell   *w rsf*   *r*4   Harringay, London
Nov 23   Eddie Keith   *w rsf*   *r*1   Manor Place Baths, London
Dec 7   Denny Ball   *w ko*   *r*3   Harringay, London

1955
Jan 27   Colin Strauch   *w rsf*   *r*1   Royal Albert Hall, London
Feb 8   Cliff Purnell   *w pts*   6*r*   Harringay, London
Mar 8   Hugh Ferns   *w dis*   *r*12   Earls Court, London
Mar 19   Joe Crickmar   *w rtd*   *r*5   Empress Hall, London
Apr 18   Joe Bygraves   *w pts*   8*r*   Manor Place Baths, London
Apr 26   Uber Bacilieri   *l rsf*   *r*2   Harringay, London
June 6   Ron Harman   *w rsf*   *r*7   Nottingham
Sept 13   Uber Bacilieri   *w ko*   *r*7   White City, London
Nov 15   Joe Erskine   *l pts*   10*r*   Harringay, London
(*British heavyweight title eliminator*)

179

1956
Feb 28   Maurice Mols   *w rsf*   *r*4   Royal Albert Hall, London
May 1   Brian London   *w rsf*   *r*1   Empress Hall, London
June 26   Giannino Luise   *w rsf r*7   Wembley, London
Sept 7   Peter Bates   *l rtd*   *r*5   Manchester

1957
Feb 19   Joe Bygraves   *l ko*   *r*9   Earls Court, London
   (*British Empire heavyweight title*)
May 19   Ingemar Johansson   *l ko*   *r*5   Stockholm
   (*European heavyweight title*)
Sept 17   Joe Erskine   *l pts*   15*r*   Harringay, London
   (*British heavyweight title*)
Nov 16   Hans Kalbfell   *w pts*   10*r*   Dortmund

1958
Jan 1   Heinz Neuhaus   *dr*   10*r*   Dormund
Apr 19   Erich Schoeppner   *l dis*   *r*6   Frankfurt
Sept 3   Dick Richardson   *w rsf*   *r*5   Porthcawl
Oct 14   Zora Folley   *w pts*   10*r*   Wembley, London

1959
Jan 12   Brian London   *w pts*   15*r*   Earls Court, London
   (*British and Empire heavyweight titles*)
Aug 26   Gawie de Klerk   *w rsf*   *r*5   Porthcawl
   (*British Empire heavyweight title*)
Nov 17   Joe Erskine   *w rsf*   *r*12   Earls Court, London
   (*British and Empire heavyweight titles*)

1960
Sept 13   Roy Harris   *w pts*   10*r*   Wembley, London
Dec 6   Alex Miteff   *w pts*   10*r*   Wembley, London

1961
Mar 21   Joe Erskine   *w rtd*   *r*5   Wembley, London
   (*British and Empire heavyweight titles*)
Dec 5   Zora Folley   *l ko*   *r*2   Wembley, London

180

1962
Jan 23   Tony Hughes   *w rtd*   r5   Wembley, London
Feb 26   Wayne Bethea   *w pts*   10r   Manchester
Apr 2   Joe Erskine   *w rsf*   r9   Nottingham
   (*British and Empire heavyweight titles*)

1963
Mar 26   Dick Richardson   *w ko*   r5   Wembley, London
   (*British and Empire heavyweight titles*)
June 18   Cassius Clay   *l rsf*   r5   Wembley, London

1964
Feb 24   Brian London   *w pts*   15r   Manchester
   (*British Empire and vacant European heavyweight titles*)
Sept 9   *European heavyweight title declared vacant*
   because of Cooper's inability, through injury, to defend it
   against Karl Mildenberger.
Nov 16   Roger Rischer   *l pts*   10r   Royal Albert Hall,
   London

1965
Jan 12   Dick Wipperman   *w rsf*   r5   Royal Albert Hall,
   London
Apr 20   Chip Johnson   *w ko*   r1   Wolverhampton
June 15   Johnny Prescott   *w rtd*   r10   Birmingham
   (*British and Empire heavyweight titles*)
Oct 19   Amos Johnson   *l pts*   10r   Wembley, London

1966
Jan 25   Hubert Hilton   *w rsf*   r2   Olympia, London
Feb 16   Jefferson Davis   *w ko*   r1   Wolverhampton
May 21   Muhammad Ali (Cassius Clay)   *l rsf*   r6
   Arsenal Stadium, London
   (*World heavyweight title*)
Sept 20   Floyd Patterson   *l ko*   r4   Wembley, London

1967
Apr 17   Boston Jacobs   *w pts*   10r   Leicester
June 13   Jack Bodell   *w rsf*   r2   Wolverhampton
   (*British and Empire heavyweight titles*)
Nov 7   Billy Walker   *w rsf*   r6   Wembley, London
   (*British and Empire heavyweight titles*)

1968
Sept 18   Karl Mildenberger   *w dis*   r8   Wembley,
London
(*European heavyweight title*)

1969
Mar 13   Piero Tomasoni   *w ko*   r5   Rome
(*European heavyweight title*)
May 28   *Gave up British and Empire heavyweight titles in
protest*
Oct 9   *Gave up European heavyweight title because of
injury*

1970
Mar 24   Jack Bodell   *w pts*   15r   Wembley, London
(*British and Commonwealth heavyweight titles*)
Nov 10   José Urtain   *w rsf*   r9   Wembley, London
(*European heavyweight title*)

1971
Mar 16   Joe Bugner   *l pts*   15r   Wembley, London
(*British, European and Commonwealth heavyweight
titles*)

INDEX

HC : Henry Cooper

José Torres

... Sting Like A Bee

'Outstanding . . . this is the best book on Muhammad Ali yet, and it will take some beating'

Harry Carpenter, Books and Bookmen

'The book is a remarkable book and the writer a remarkable writer. Booze and tobacco I constantly run away from as damaging, corrupting things. For a long time I have been thinking the same thing about boxing and trying to push it away. Then up comes a book like José Torres' *Sting Like a Bee*, and all the smell and sweat and the evil magic is back'

Eamonn Andrews, Punch

'A knockout . . . Torres gives electrifying accounts of Ali's battles in and out of the ring'

Daily Mirror

'The book promises to tell 'the Muhammad Ali story'. It does that and much more. José Torres was himself light-heavyweight champion of no mean accomplishment but now he has done for boxing with the pen something which he never excelled at in the ring'

Michael Foot, Evening Standard

The Muhammad Ali Story

Preface by Norman Mailer
Epilogue by Budd Schulberg

SPORTING CORONET

	JOSE TORRES	
☐ 16472 7	Sting Like A Bee	30p
	TOMMY ARMOUR	
☐ 01044 4	How to Play Your Best Golf All the Time	30p
	LEONARD BARDEN	
☐ 02869 6	The Guardian Chess Book	30p
	IRA CORN JNR	
☐ 17314 9	Play Bridge With The Aces	40p
	ERIC DOMINY	
☐ 14813 6	Karate	30p
	ROBERT HARBIN	
☐ 10902 5	Origami 1	30p
☐ 15384 9	Origami 2	30p
☐ 16655 X	Origami 3	30p
	HENRY LONGHURST	
☐ 02439 9	How to get started in Golf	30p
	JACK NICKLAUS	
☐ 04348 2	The Best Way to Better Golf No. 1	25p
☐ 10539 9	The Best Way to Better Golf No. 2	25p
☐ 15475 6	The Best Way to Better Golf No. 3	25p
	STANLEY PHILLIPS	
☐ 03827 6	Stamp Collecting	30p
	IAN PROCTOR	
☐ 03781 4	Racing Dinghy Handling	40p
	FALCON TRAVIS	
☐ 04143 9	Camping And Hiking	25p

All these books are available at your bookshop or newsagent, or can be ordered direct from the publisher. Just tick the titles you want and fill in the form below.

CORONET BOOKS, P.O. Box 11, Falmouth, Cornwall.

Please send cheque or postal order. No currency, and allow the following for postage and packing:

1 book – 10p, 2 books – 15p, 3 books – 20p, 4–5 books – 25p, 6–9 books – 4p per copy, 10–15 books – 2½p per copy, over 30 books free within the U.K.
Overseas – please allow **10p** for the first book and 5p per copy for each additional book.

Name...

Address...

....